A

Major Money Decisions

Copyright ©2001
The Kiplinger Washington Editors, Inc.
All rights reserved.

No part of this book may be reproduced or transmitted in any form or by any means, electronic or mechanical, including photocopying, recording or by an information storage and retrieval system, without the written permission of the Publisher, except where permitted by law.

Executive Producers:
Thomas L. Conrad
Conrad & Associates, Inc.

Frank B. Phillippi
The Kiplinger Washington Editors, Inc.

Cover and text designed by Utopia Communications Group.
ISBN: 0-938721-94-1
Manufactured in the United States of America
Second edition: 2001

Major Money Decisions is available in bulk quantities at discounts. For more information, contact:
Conrad & Associates, Inc.
10415 Stapleford Hall Drive
Potomac, Maryland 20854
301-983-6417
800-553-0504

This package has been designed as an educational tool. While providing information, it is not intended to provide advice for specific individuals and should not be relied upon as the basis for investment or legal decisions. The authors and producers disclaim all responsibility for misunderstandings and specific positions taken by the viewers and readers of this product.

Acknowledgments

The information contained in *Major Money Decisions* is based on the book *Kiplinger's Practical Guide to Your Money,* by Ted Miller. Miller, who was editor of *Kiplinger's Personal Finance* magazine for 13 years, is also the author of *Kiplinger's Practical Guide to Investing.*

Jennifer Robinson edited the original edition of the guidebook and Allison Leopold proofread it; Norma Shaw provided the updated information for the second edition. Frank Phillippi produced the videotape. Thanks also to Alan Weiss, Deborah Gobble and Tania Wilk at Alan Weiss Productions.

Finally, special thanks go to the families and individuals who shared their experiences and insights with our viewers.

Contents

Chapter 1: Take Charge of Your Money 3

Chapter 2: Managing Credit 17

Chapter 3: Protecting Your Life 35

Chapter 4: How to Have Investing Smarts........................46

Chapter 5: Buying a Home 56

Chapter 6: Insuring Your Home 85

Chapter 7: Buying a Car 95

Chapter 8: Insuring Your Car 111

Chapter 9: Paying for College 124

Chapter 10: A Comfortable Retirement 138

Chapter 11: Passing it On 146

Chapter 1

Take Charge of Your Money

The world is mesmerized by money. A rack full of newspapers and a truckload of newsletters devote themselves entirely to chronicling the use and abuse of money. Cable TV beams money-related programming day and night. The Internet is jammed with money-minded Web sites. Scribes pen countless books about money. Money is a top-ten topic of family conversation, too. It's a well-reported fact that married couples fight more about money than about sex. A recent edition of *Bartlett's Familiar Quotations* lists 92 entries for the word *money*, a mere 25 for *sex*.

Considering that the subject occupies so much of our time and attention, isn't it amazing that so many people have barely a clue about how to handle their own money? Amazing maybe, but no mystery: Americans typically manage to navigate 12, 16 or more years of very fine formal education without ever learning how to balance a checkbook, size up a stock or resist a fast-talking salesman of bad financial ideas.

The purpose of this guidebook is to fill in the blanks, by suggesting ways to use the money you have to live better today and build a more secure future at the same time. Along the way it will attempt to explain many things (some of which you will already be familiar with, or think you are), and help you tackle life's big financial decisions. It's written with the expectation that you'll skip the subjects you know in order to concentrate on the ones you don't know.

Where Are You Now?

If you've been around awhile and feel comfortably on top of your regular income and outgo, then maybe you can safely skip this chapter. On the other hand, if you have to admit that you're barely making it from payday to payday, or if you're not exactly drowning but have the distinct feeling that you're treading water while others swim merrily by, then here is where you'll find the means to get moving.

One thing you need to do is take a financial inventory. That means sorting out the money and other assets that are all yours from those that someone has a claim on—in other words, finding out what you *own* and what you *owe*. This isn't hard to do. You add up the value of everything you own, then you subtract from it the total of all your debts. The result is your net worth, and the form on page 10 will walk you through the steps.

Before you check out the form, though, it will be helpful to perform another little piece of self-analysis. Taking some time to record what you do with the money that passes through your hands on a day-to-day basis will pay off in valuable information about the state of your financial affairs. It's the first step in getting them under control.

If you haven't been paying much attention to where your money goes, fill in the cash-flow form on page 7. You'll have exact figures for some expenses—mortgage or rent, for example, and insurance premiums—and you can estimate others on a monthly basis. Go over your canceled checks, paid bills and credit card statements. Hang on to cash-register receipts from stores, cleaners, gas stations and restaurants. The more actual expenditures you can pinpoint, the more you'll know about your spending habits when you're through.

No matter how this exercise comes out, you're going to be confronted with the evidence of your spending and forced to make some judgments about it. You'll find yourself in one of three situations.

Are income and expenditures roughly in balance?

Making it from one year to the next without getting into a hole may be something of a feat these days, but before you start patting yourself on the back, check your totals again. How much did you put into savings compared with what you spent on recreation, gifts or clothing? Out-of-whack entries in those or other categories of discretionary spending could mean trouble's brewing. There's more to good money management than balancing the books. You have to balance your priorities, too.

Did you make more than you spent?
This isn't necessarily a good sign, either. Because your cash-flow statement includes savings and investments, you shouldn't have any money left over. What may at first look like a surplus is probably just a failure to remember some spending. Go over the numbers again.

Did you spend more than you made?
This is the clearest sign of trouble ahead. You've either been dipping into savings, borrowing money or buying on credit. You can get away with it for a while, and there are times when it's smart to borrow or when you have no choice. But as a regular practice, it's bad money management that will cost you in the long run.

Go over your cash-flow statement carefully, looking for places where your money might be dribbling away. As you proceed with this chapter, you should begin to spot some ways to plug the leaks.

How Much Are You Worth?

Now you have a picture of how you're handling the money that comes your way on a regular basis. But performing a cash-flow analysis for a single year doesn't give you much information about the cumulative impact on your financial worth of all the cash that's been flowing through your hands day after day for all of your adult life. A net-worth statement will show you this, and a form for creating one is on page 10. Here's how to use it.

Add up assets
Start with cash: what you have on hand, what's in your checking account and what you may have squirreled away elsewhere. Next list money in savings accounts and certificates of deposit. (If you own U.S. savings bonds and want to be finicky about it, check their current values with a bank or go online (www.publicdebt.treas.gov) to get them. But you could spend the better part of a day at that little exercise if you own more than, say, a dozen bonds bought over a period of years. You might settle for a ballpark estimate of the value, which is somewhere between what you paid for them (half their face value) and what they're worth today.

Premium payments on a whole-life insurance policy add to your net worth by increasing the policy's cash value (the amount you'd get if you cashed it in). Your insurance agent or a table in the policy can tell you the current cash value. Ditto for the surrender value of any annuities you own.

Settling on figures to enter as the current value of your pension and profit-sharing plans is tricky. A program that will provide you with retirement income is surely an important asset, but it's difficult (although by no means impossible) to put a present-day dollar value on income you're supposed to receive in the future. For purposes of this statement, include in your net worth only the amount you could withdraw in cash if you quit your job today. Your personnel office should be able to provide that figure. If you have an individual retirement account, 401(k) plan or Keogh, list its current balance.

Your home is likely to be your biggest asset, so it's especially important that the value you assign to it be accurate. Don't list what it cost you or take a wild guess at its present value. Check around to find out what similar homes in your area are selling for or have sold for recently, or ask a real estate agent for an estimate of current market value. Try to get reliable estimates of the value of any other real estate or business interests you own, too.

The current market value of financial assets such as stocks, bonds and mutual funds is easy to find in the newspaper or on recent statements from your funds or broker.

You can get a good idea of what your car is worth by consulting a car-price guide, such as the *Kelley Blue Book* (www.kbb.com) or the *N.A.D.A. Official Used Car Guide*, published by the National Automobile Dealers Association (www.nada.org). Banks that make auto loans usually have copies of those guides, as do many public libraries. For help in putting a value on a boat, motorcycle or other vehicle, contact a dealer or check the prices of comparable models in the classified ads.

Ballpark figures will do for the value of household furnishings, appliances and other personal belongings. It's best to be conservative in your estimates. One conservative approach is to guesstimate that what's inside your home is worth about 20% to 30% of the value of the home itself. Or make your own item-by-item estimate, then slash it by 50%. Use estimated market value (not purchase price) of antiques, furs, jewelry, and stamp or coin collections.

Look at liabilities

Filling out this portion of the form may be painful, but it shouldn't be difficult. Most liabilities are obvious, and whoever you owe probably reminds you of the debt on a regular basis.

Start with current bills—what you owe the doctor and the plumber, this month's phone bill and credit card charges. Next, list the balance due on every credit card and installment debt. There's a separate line on the form for your car loan and another one for taxes coming due. Your home mortgage is probably your largest single lia-

Your Cash Flow

Income	Total for Year	Monthly Average
Take-home pay	$ _____	$ _____
Dividends, capital gains, interest	_____	_____
Bonuses	_____	_____
Other	_____	_____
Total income	$ _____	$ _____

Expenditures		
Mortgage or rent	$ _____	$ _____
Taxes not withheld from pay	_____	_____
Food	_____	_____
Utilities and fuel	_____	_____
Insurance premiums	_____	_____
Household maintenance	_____	_____
Auto (gas, oil, maintenance, repairs)	_____	_____
Other transportation (bus, parking)	_____	_____
Loan payment	_____	_____
Credit card interest	_____	_____
Medical bills not covered by insurance	_____	_____
Clothing and care	_____	_____
Savings and investments	_____	_____
Charity	_____	_____
Recreation and entertainment	_____	_____
Miscellaneous	_____	_____
Total expenditures	$ _____	$ _____
SUMMARY		
Total income	$ _____	$ _____
Minus total expenditures	_____	_____
surplus (+) or deficit (–)	$ _____	$ _____

bility, and the year-end statement from the lender should show exactly how much you still owe on it. On other lines, list every debt you can think of because whatever you owe is a liability that diminishes your net worth.

Behold the bottom line

Now it's time to fill in the bottom line. If you sold all your assets and paid all your debts, what would be left over? That's your net worth.

It's probably not what you'd like it to be. It's even possible that it's a negative number, especially if you're young and just took out a big mortgage on a house and a big loan on a car. But don't worry—be happy, because you've just taken the first step toward starting or revising a budget that can show you ways to beef up your assets and trim your liabilities. Before you continue, you need to set some goals.

No Money Left to Save

Q: I'd like to start saving some money, but after I've made the mortgage payment, the car payment, bought the groceries and had a little fun (and I do mean a little), all the money is gone. Is there any hope for people like me?

A: There are at least a couple of avenues you can investigate.
Do you get an income-tax refund each year? If so, take a trip to your company's human resources office and adjust your withholding to reflect more closely the taxes you'll owe for the year. If you tend to get a $500 refund, you can increase your take-home pay by more than $40 a month by changing your withholding.
When was the last time you reshopped your homeowners and auto insurance policies? Premiums charged by different companies for the same level of coverage in the same city can vary by hundreds of dollars a year—money that you can convert to a savings account.
There's one more step: When you've freed up the cash from these other sources, authorize your bank to take it out of your checking account automatically each month and transfer it to savings. Out of sight, out of mind—until you begin to notice how the money in your account is adding up.

Getting Ready to Set Goals

You probably don't expect to attain great wealth in your lifetime. Simple financial security would do, if only you knew what that meant. It's a slippery notion, all right, but it does have a few characteristics you can grab on to.

You need a steady source of income. This comes from your job, or your business if you're self-employed, or investments if you're fortunate and alert. Future income is the bedrock on which financial security is built.

You need financial reserves. Cars break down, household appliances wear out, roofs spring leaks. Kids aspire to college educations, and someday you'll want to retire. These are expenses you have to provide for with savings and investments.

You need protection against financial catastrophes. In a word, this means insurance. You need it in sufficient amounts to cover your life, your health, your ability to earn an income, and your family and your possessions. Without insurance, the best-laid financial plans can be wiped out in an instant.

You need to get further ahead each year. If you stand pat, even modest inflation will grind away at your financial reserves just as surely as if you were spending the money. To stay ahead of the cost of living, you have to be alert for opportunities to make your money grow.

These things don't come to you by accident. You have to go after them, and that means setting some goals.

How to Set Financial Goals

The most important step toward financial security is to translate it into your own terms. What, exactly, are your personal financial goals? If you have trouble sorting them out, try classifying them as either *wants* or *needs*. Go a step further and add long-term or short-term to the description. Now you have some useful labels you can apply to your priorities.

Say you're going to *need* a new car soon. Gathering the money for a down payment without borrowing or dipping into savings would be a short-term need. Let's call it, and other short-term needs such as your daughter's braces or a new winter coat, priority number one.

Your Net Worth

Assets
Cash in checking accounts	$ _____
Cash in savings accounts	_____
Certificates of deposit	_____
U.S. savings bonds (current value)	_____
Cash value of life insurance	_____
Equity in pension, 401(k) and profit-sharing plans	_____
Market value of IRA or Keogh plan	_____
Surrender value of annuities	_____
Market value of house or apartment	_____
Market value of other real estate	_____
Market value of securities	
Stocks	_____
Bonds	_____
Mutual fund shares	_____
Other	_____
Current value of durable possessions	
Automobiles	_____
Household furnishings	_____
Household appliances and equipment	_____
Furs and jewelry	_____
Precious metals	_____
Collectibles	_____
Recreation and hobby equipment	_____
Loans receivable	_____
Interest in a business	_____
Other assets	_____
Total Assets	$ _____

Liabilities
Current bills outstanding	$ _____
Credit card balances	_____
Car loans	_____
Taxes due	_____
Balance due on mortgages	_____
Other loans	_____
Other liabilities	_____

Summary
Total Liabilities	$ _____
Assets	$ _____
Minus Liabilities	− _____
Net Worth	$ _____

Longer-term needs, such as contributions to a retirement fund, can get priority two. That vacation in Bermuda next spring is a short-term *want*—priority three. The 42-foot sailboat you'd like to own before too many years go by is a long-term want, so it gets a four.

You could shift priorities around, of course, and use lots more numbers. Actual goals and their priorities will vary with your circumstances. The important thing is to give serious thought to your goals and try to anticipate the expenses coming up, whether they're close at hand or several years away.

Choose goals you can get excited about, because that will make you more determined to reach them. "Financial security" sounds good, for instance, but it's hard to quantify. It needs some skin and bones. Define what it means to you. How about this? "I want to own a million dollars' worth of stocks by the time I'm 50." Or this: "We want to retire to Arizona in ten years with enough money to buy a house near Phoenix and enough income to travel in Europe for a month each year." Now you've got goals you can put a future price on, and that price can be translated into a savings and investment plan that you can start today. Put your goals in writing; that makes for a great motivational tool.

The trouble is, exciting goals and good intentions need cash to back them up. That's where budgeting comes in. It's your best bet for distributing your limited resources among competing goals.

Nitty-Gritty Budgeting

Think of your budget as a planning device, a means of setting and reaching your goals. You project future expenditures (including savings), record them when they're made, and see whether your projections were any good. If they aren't, you adjust your planning or your spending, whichever is out of line.

You'll find a suggested budget format on pages 14 and 15. There's space there for a month's expenditures. Use that format as a model to make your own budget sheets, or make copies of those two pages to give you space for more months.

Use the record of last year's spending that you compiled on page 7 as the basis for the coming year's budget projections. Work only a couple of months ahead at first, until you get the hang of it. Then you can budget further ahead. After a while you'll want to apply the same principles to long-term goal setting by forecasting the growth of your net worth and all the little pieces that compose it. Then you can keep track of the progress you're making by comparing each year's projected growth with the actual results.

Fixed Spending

Some of your projections will be easy: You know what your mortgage or rent payments will be in the months ahead. Same for car payments and the premiums coming due on insurance policies. So why budget for them? Because by recording these and other fixed expenditures as monthly outgo, you can see at a glance how much of your income is committed to current or future expenses. That should stop you from spending it on something else.

Variable Spending

Here you'll keep track of the items over which you have some degree of control. This section is the place to test your cost-cutting skills. Watch for patterns that may signal trouble. If the "miscellaneous" line keeps growing bigger, for instance, your recordkeeping may be careless.

Plugging the Holes in Your Budget

One good reason to endure the occasional drudgery of budgeting is that it alerts you to trouble while you still have time to do something about it. You're forced to find out why your expenditures are climbing and to take action. If the electric or gas bill is higher because the rates were raised, you'll have to revise your monthly forecasts for that budget item and figure out whether other items need to be cut to pay for it. If rates haven't risen, maybe it's time to discourage the kids from taking such long showers two or three times a day.

Sometimes a budget flashes danger signals that are more difficult to interpret. If you start picking up distress signals, run your budget through these checks:

Are you buying too much on credit?

Perhaps you got in this fix because you didn't watch what was going on. Examine budget categories where spending overshot allocations, paying particular attention to your credit card statements. The finance charges they generate could be enough to foul up your estimates.

Are you behind the times?

You may be in trouble not because of unnecessary spending but because your necessary spending now costs more. This is a common experience, and people who budget sometimes have trouble coping with it because they estimate spending on the basis of prices in effect at the time the budget is drawn up. You should revise your budget from time to time throughout the year to keep it in touch with reality.

Did you create a straitjacket?

Consider the couple who thought they were doing fine without a budget of any kind, until their checks suddenly began bouncing all over town. With their two-salary income, they told each other, there was simply no excuse for such embarrassment. So they vowed to budget, and for the first time ever they sat down to list their normal expenses and match them against their normal income.

To their delight, they found that not only was there enough money to go around but also that it would be perfectly realistic to fund a savings program, which they had talked about but never started. They promptly drew up a budget that included a heroic chunk of savings each month, then happily set forth on their road to affluence.

Or so they thought. In their enthusiasm they had been both too ambitious and too rigid. They had tried to shovel too much into savings. They budgeted every penny of the remainder but neglected to allow for the unforeseen expenses that are too petty to budget for but add up nevertheless.

Moral: Allow yourself leeway. Better to budget a bit too much in a few categories (certainly including *miscellaneous* or *contingencies*) than to end each month robbing Peter to pay Paul. The purpose of a budget is not to make impossible dreams come true but to make attainable goals come more easily.

Are you doing somebody else's thing?

Years ago, the Bureau of Labor Statistics invented a hypothetical urban family of four, and it periodically computed itemized budgets for this family, just to see how much it was costing them to live.

Newspapers and magazines faithfully reported changes in this budget and editorial writers clucked sympathetically as costs rose to squeeze this imaginary mom and pop and their imaginary children. But if by wild chance yours happened to be an urban family of four with precisely the same income, it is likely your budget would have looked very little like the BLS version. (And indeed, the agency eventually abandoned this exercise.)

A Budget for Today and Tomorrow

Use this format to get on top of your living costs by projecting expenditures in various categories. Then record what you actually spend and see how close your projections came to reality. Do this month-by-month to begin with, and you'll see where you need to plug the leaks in your spending.

Income
Take-home pay   _____
Other (specify)   _____
Total $ _____

Fixed Expenditures	**Projected**	**Actual**	**(+) or (−)**
Mortgage or rent	$ _____	$ _____	$ _____
Taxes not withheld from pay	_____	_____	_____
Installment and credit-card payments	_____	_____	_____
	_____	_____	_____
	_____	_____	_____
	_____	_____	_____
Insurance Premiums			
Life	_____	_____	_____
Auto	_____	_____	_____
Home	_____	_____	_____
Health	_____	_____	_____
Other	_____	_____	_____
Savings/Investments			
Vacation fund	_____	_____	_____
Emergency fund	_____	_____	_____
Investment fund	_____	_____	_____
Retirement or 401(k)	_____	_____	_____
Other (specify)	_____	_____	_____
Subtotal	$ _____	$ _____	$ _____

Your budget is unique to you and your family. It embodies private decisions you make about how you'll allocate your resources. Behind those decisions are your own goals, aspirations, values, hopes, anxieties, lifestyle, commitments and, to an important degree, even the expectations of people whose expectations you regard as worthy of honoring.

In short, you can't live by somebody else's budget. Yours has to be tailored to your measure, by you.

Variable Expenditures	Projected	Actual	(+) or (−)
Food and beverages	$	$	$
Fuel and utilities			
Gas or oil			
Electricity			
Telephone			
Water and sewer			
Household operation and maintenance			
Automobile			
Gas and oil			
Repairs			
Public transportation			
Clothing			
Mom			
Dad			
Kids			
Pocket money			
Mom			
Dad			
Kids			
Personal care (haircuts, etc.)			
Recreation, entertainment			
Medical and dental			
Charity			
Special expenses (tuition, alimony, etc.)			
Miscellaneous			
Subtotal	$	$	$
Plus fixed expenditures	$	$	$
Total	$	$	$

Most people approach budgeting by listing first the expenditures about which they feel they have no choice whatsoever. If anything is left over, only then do they consider expenditures they might make from free choice. Budgeting doesn't have to proceed this grimly, however. A few people begin at the other end. First they put down their desired goals, such as "enough money to buy a 36-foot sailboat by 2005." Then they budget to attain *those* goals before distributing the remainder among items most people would rank as first-order necessities—shelter, food, clothing and the like.

Granted, this doesn't always work. It takes a strong-minded individual to budget wishes first, and needs later. But it *can* work, which just shows how highly personal the whole budgeting process can be.

Chapter 2

Managing Credit

How much debt is too much? It depends. That's not the answer you wanted, perhaps, but it's the only sensible one: It depends on how easily you can repay the money and what you borrowed it for in the first place.

A long-standing rule of thumb holds that monthly payments on debts (not including a home mortgage, which is really more of an investment) shouldn't exceed 20% of take-home pay. The closer you get to that 20% ceiling, the greater your risk of over-indebtedness.

Rules of thumb can be useful, but don't count on this one to keep you out of trouble. It says nothing about your total financial obligations or your level of income. If you take home $4,000 a month and live in a paid-up house, you can more easily afford $800 in monthly credit card bills than if you take home $2,000 and have to shell out $400 on top of the rent. Whatever you make and whatever you owe, you probably have a pretty good idea of whether you're heading for trouble. Too much debt flashes these warning signals:

- **You find it more and more difficult each month** to make ends meet.

- **It's taking extraordinary effort to pay your ordinary expenses.** Perhaps you rely heavily on overtime pay or income from moonlighting, just to pay the rent and buy the groceries.

- **You've picked up the habit of paying only the minimum** due on your credit card bills each month, and sometimes you juggle payments, stalling one company to pay another.

- **You can't save even small amounts** and don't have enough set aside to get you through such setbacks as a pay cut, an unexpected car repair or an emergency visit to your parents.

Chapter Two • **17**

Even if you seem to be getting along fine, you should examine your debt situation occasionally. For instance, you might take a stab at filling out the debt worksheet on the opposite page. Use your checkbook and credit card statements to find information on expenses. Where you have to estimate, be realistic, not optimistic. (If you filled out the cash-flow form on page 7, this form will be easy.)

Pay attention not only to how much you have to pay each month but also to how many months into the future you'll be stuck with those payments. If you quit using credit today, for example, how long would it take to pay off your non-mortgage debts? Six months? A year? Longer?

The worksheet shows you the maximum amount you can afford to pay on debts each month. How close you want to come to that limit is your call. Base it on these considerations: How secure is your income? Can you count on raises every year? How far down the road have payments on today's debts pushed the starting date for an investment program?

Set a debt limit that considers what you can afford today and, just as important, what today's obligations are borrowing from tomorrow. If debt is a problem, solving it should go right to the top of your list of financial priorities.

How to Get Out of Debt

Whatever the elusive "proper" level of debt may be, a lot of people are exceeding it. Despite generally widespread prosperity in recent years, Americans have gone broke in record numbers, filing for personal bankruptcy like never before. If you see such drastic action looming in your future, better to take some steps now before your credit rating is ruined.

Roll Your Debts Into a Lower-Rate Loan

Perhaps you can reduce your monthly payments by combining your major debts into a longer-term loan at a lower interest rate. This can be an especially rewarding strategy for credit card debt, which clobbers you with the highest interest around. A home-equity loan or a loan from a 401(k) plan at work may make sense. The rate will be lower, and you'll reduce the number of checks you have to write each month. But before you take this step, read the section about home-equity loans on page 29.

Sizing Up Your Debts

Use this worksheet to set a personal debt limit.

1. Figure your monthly income

Your take-home pay	$ _____
Spouse's take-home pay	_____
Other regular income	_____
A. Total monthly income	$ _____

2. Figure your monthly expenses

Other regular income	$ _____
Rent or mortgage	_____
Food	_____
Utilities	_____
Savings and investments	_____
Insurance	_____
Charitable contributions	_____
Transportation and auto maintenance	_____
Entertainment	_____
All other	_____
B. Monthly expenses	$ _____

3. Figure your annual expenses

Taxes (not deducted from pay or included in mortgage payment)	$ _____
Insurance (not paid monthly)	_____
Medical and dental bills	_____
School costs	_____
Major purchases and repairs	_____
Vacation	_____
Clothing	_____
All other	_____
C. Total annual expenses	$ _____
D. Total to set aside monthly for annual expenses	$ _____

(Divide C by 12 to find the amount (D) to set aside to cover these expenses)

E. Total monthly expenses (B+D) $ _____

4. Figure your payments on current debts. Monthly expenses (credit cards, car loan, etc)

	Monthly Payment	Balance	Months Left
_____	$ _____	_____	_____
_____	_____	_____	_____
_____	_____	_____	_____

F. Total payments on current debt $ _____
G. Total monthly outlay (E+F) $ _____

5. Compare total on line (G) to monthly income (A) $ _____

Chapter Two • **19**

Switch to a Lower-Rate Credit Card
Credit card offers are everywhere, and card issuers will gladly arrange for you to roll balances on existing cards into a new account with them provided your credit rating is still good (see below). Just make sure that you don't sign up for a low introductory rate that converts to a high rate after only a few months.

Check Your Credit Record
You can get a free credit report if you've been denied credit in the past 60 days. The credit-reporting agencies are Equifax (800–685–1111), Experian (888-397-3742) and Trans Union (800–916–8800). If you live in Georgia, Maryland, Massachusetts or Vermont, the report is always free, by state law. Also, federal law requires the credit-reporting firms to provide free reports to people who are out of work and looking, who are on welfare, or who believe that their credit record is inaccurate because of fraud. Otherwise, there is a small fee.

Confess to Your Creditors
If you know things are going to get worse before they get better, call your creditors and spill the beans. Tell them you that can't pay on time but are determined to pay them back. Could they possibly stretch out the payments for you? Some will do it, and some will even waive interest and late fees for a while. If you get such an agreement, follow up with a letter to the company describing the terms you discussed. This protects you later if the company decides to change its mind.

Know Your Rights
See the section on credit rights later on page 32.

Get Some Help
If things are looking bleak and you can't handle it alone, consider calling the nonprofit National Foundation for Credit Counseling (800–388–2227), which operates more than 2,000 local offices. The national number will put you in touch with the local office, where counselors can help you set up a repayment program and negotiate with creditors for reduced monthly payments and lower—or even waived—finance charges. The CCCS then helps you set up a budget that calls for you to make one monthly payment to the service, which parcels it out to your creditors. There may be a small fee involved.

Why would creditors agree to such a program? For one thing, half a loaf is better than none: This way they are assured of getting at least some of their money from borrowers who might otherwise pay back nothing. In fact, creditors are so anxious to cooperate that they often pay the CCCS a percentage of the money they collect. This is a next-to-last resort, but you said you were desperate, right?

Declare Bankruptcy

The absolutely last resort is bankruptcy, which for individuals usually means looking for protection under either Chapter 7 or Chapter 13 of the bankruptcy code. Most people choose Chapter 7, probably because it permits you to erase virtually all your debts even if you're capable of repaying some of them. This irks creditors no end. They believe that many people who file Chapter 7 have income enough to qualify under Chapter 13 instead. Chapter 13 filers agree to repay their debts over three to five years. If you find yourself considering filing for bankruptcy, think again. You shouldn't take this step before you have exhausted the options outlined above. A bankruptcy stays in your credit file for seven to ten years. You may be able to qualify for new credit during that time, but not on terms you'll like.

Finding the Best Credit Deals

The best way to stay out of credit trouble is to borrow sparingly. The second-best way is to know what you're talking about and what you're hearing when you do borrow.

When you're shopping for the best credit deal, whether it's a plastic card or a paper mortgage, the only basis of comparison to use is the annual percentage rate (APR). It is figured on the size of the unpaid balance, which shrinks as you pay off the loan. The federal Truth in Lending Act requires that lenders use APR when quoting interest rates, so that you can be sure you're comparing apples with apples. If the rate you're quoted sounds suspiciously low or if the lender quotes you only a monthly dollar payment, make sure to get the APR. If you're still unsure of a rate you're quoted, check it with another lender.

There are different kinds of credit, different sources of credit and different prices for credit. It pays you, literally, to know the difference. Here are some credit rules of thumb that *are* worth remembering when you're in the market for a loan.

- **Finance companies charge higher interest rates** than banks, which generally charge higher rates than credit unions.
- **Secured loans**—that is, loans backed by some sort of collateral, which the lender takes if you default—cost less than unsecured loans.
- **Some kinds of collateral provide better security than others.** For example, you'll get a lower rate on a new-car loan than on a used-car loan, and you'll get a lower rate on a first mortgage than on a second mortgage.
- **The longer the term of a loan, the lower the monthly payments**—but the more interest you'll pay before it's over.

Credit à la Card

When discussing the kind of credit that comes with a plastic card, the first distinction to make is between *charge* cards and *credit* cards. American Express and Diners Club are *charge* cards. You are expected to pay their bills in full within a specified time period. If you don't, you'll be penalized (more about them later).

Visa, MasterCard, Discover and other *credit* cards don't necessarily encourage you to pay your bill in full because they automatically charge interest—lots of interest—on the unpaid balance. The smart way to use credit cards is to use them as if they are charge cards: Pay your bill in full each month. Often the card will allow a grace period of 25 to 30 days from the date you're billed before interest begins accruing. If you pay the bill in full before the grace period runs out, you get, in effect, a free loan. Deals like this make some credit cards the closest you'll ever come to free money. And if you make your purchases right after your billing date, you can stretch the term of this free-money period to nearly two months.

Unfortunately, grace periods aren't universally available. Many card issuers start charging interest from the date of a purchase if you carry over a balance from the previous month. This system is also popular among department stores that issue their own credit cards. Nevertheless, you can still keep the cost of your multipurpose cards under control if you keep an eye on the charges you're paying.

Compare cards on the following features.

Annual fees

These charges, if any, range from an average of $20 for the run-of-the-mill Visa or MasterCard, to $50 or so for a gold card. As the credit card business has grown more competitive, card issuers have shown a willingness to drop the annual fee for customers they'd like to keep. If you think your fee is too high, ask to have it waived. Explain that you've been a good customer and you don't see why you should have to pay a fee when so many cards are available without one. If you have been a good customer, odds are good that the company will drop the fee.

Fees for "free riders"

Pay your bills on time and you pay no interest, right? Yes, but some card issuers have found a way to sock it to free riders like you, who have the audacity to pay off their balances in full before incurring any interest charges. Some simply levy a different charge, perhaps by nicking you with a small fee each time they use the card. Cardholders who run up interest charges for the month escape the fee, as do cardholders who use the card frequently (generating fees paid by the merchants who accept the card). But if you find yourself with a card like this, look for a different one.

Interest rates

Interest rates are set by the bank or savings and loan that issues your credit card, not by the card company. Issuers have to stay under the interest limits set by the state in which their headquarters are chartered. But that's rarely much comfort because the limits are often 18% to 22%, or even more. Introductory rates, which may last six months or a year, are often lower.

Other fees and charges

You will be charged interest on cash advances, a fee for paying late and a fee for exceeding your credit limit.

Protection against fraud

Plastic credit is pretty safe. If your card or your card number is used fraudulently by someone else, the law limits your liability to $50, and issuing banks often don't make customers pay even that much. If your account is used fraudulently to charge something without actually showing the card—say, if someone orders merchandise over the phone or online—you owe nothing. All this is provided you report the fraud within 60 days of the date of the statement on which it appears.

Finding the Best Credit Card Deal

The great variety of credit card fees can work to your advantage. If you aren't satisfied with the terms your card company is offering, you may be able to find a less expensive plan somewhere else. The way

---

Keep Your Interest Rate Low—
And Avoid Those Fees

Like a lot of other things in life, credit-card rules used to be simpler. But then came rebates, balance transfers and a wave of penalties for day-late and dollar-over-the-limit transgressions. Today, keeping a low interest rate, avoiding penalties and making sense of rebate programs takes a rule book worthy of Hoyle. The queries and answers below can help you make the most of the cards you hold and anticipate the aces up the issuer's sleeve.

Q: I love a good deal. To take advantage of low introductory rates, I've opened and closed a dozen accounts in the past three years. Will that hurt my credit rating?

A: There's nothing wrong with chasing teaser rates, but it's important to close your old accounts and make sure your credit report reflects that they were "closed by customer." Otherwise you could be denied a loan because you have too much available credit. In addition, some credit card issuers have begun to screen out people who jump from card to card, so you might be turned down for a card at some point. Just in case, favor cards that give you a low rate even after the introductory period is over.

Finally, keep an eye on the fine print. A few issuers have tried to impose account-closing fees, or charge a fee for using a convenience check to transfer your balance.

Q: My balance includes purchases, cash advances and balance transfers, each of which carries a different interest rate. The bank applies my payment to the transferred balance first because it has the lowest interest rate. Is there a way to apply the payment to purchases or cash advances instead?

A: Your bank's policy is common—there's no federal or state law that requires creditors to allocate your payment in any particular manner. The best way around the practice is to transfer your balance to a new card with a low interest rate for balance transfers. Then use a separate, low-rate card for new purchases and cash advances and pay off the card with the higher rate first.

Q: I signed up for a card with a 7.9% rate, and later I got a solicitation for the same card with a 5.9% rate. Can I get the lower rate?

you use your credit card should determine which pricing scheme works out best for you.

Do you pay your bill in full every month?

In this case, you don't care about the APR but still need to find an account that doesn't start charging interest from the date of purchase. Look for the longest grace period you can find.

A: Ask for it. Because it costs card issuers a lot more to acquire a new customer than to retain an old one, the lower rate is probably yours for the asking.

Q: I mailed in my credit card payment on time, but the bank says it arrived late. Can I do anything to avoid a late fee and interest?

A: A phone call may be all it takes to remove the charge, especially if you have a clean record. Or you can dispute the fee as a billing error by writing the issuer within 60 days of your statement date. (You may be able to bolster your case by finding out when your check cleared.)

If the bank won't budge, your options aren't great. You can cancel the card and refuse to pay the fee; if it shows up on your credit report, you'll want to add a notation that you dispute the entry. It might be easier to cough up the fee and let it go. But that can make matters worse, as some banks are switching customers who pay late more than once to higher interest rates.

One way to avoid the problem altogether is to use a bill-paying service, such as Quicken or CheckFree. Most guarantee that your payment will arrive on time if you send instructions four or five business days before the due date.

Q: I never got my bill this month. Am I stuck if I don't pay on time?

A: Unfortunately, yes. According to Federal Reserve regulations, banks must send you a statement at least 14 days before your payment is due. But you're still responsible for paying on time, even if the bill doesn't arrive. If you're going to move, give card issuers your new address well ahead of time.

Q: My card issuer is about to raise my interest rate. Can I ditch the card and pay off the balance over time at the current rate?

A: Usually, yes. Credit card issuers in several states (including Delaware, where many issuers are based) are required to let you pay off your balance at the old rate as long as you close the account to new charges. Even in states where there is no such law, many card issuers offer the same arrangement. But if you use the card after the new rate takes effect, you will have automatically accepted the new terms.

Q: I hadn't used my credit card for about a year when my bank suddenly canceled my account. Can a bank do that?

A: Afraid so. Even if your account is in good standing and you haven't been late with a payment even once, an issuer has the right to rescind your card. Some have even closed accounts on active customers because they incurred no fees or interest charges.

Do you carry over balances from month to month?
Then you'll be paying interest on interest. Look for the lowest interest-rate-and-fee combination.

Because both Visa and MasterCard are welcome just about anywhere credit cards are used in this country, acceptability should have nothing to do with which one you choose. Watch for special deals offered by the banks that issue these cards, and by the bankcards' most serious competitors, such as Discover and the general-purpose cards issued by airlines, phone companies and auto manufacturers. The market is awash with cards that reward customers with frequent-flier miles on selected airlines, or discounts on cars or other major purchases. Since the terms of these deals change so frequently, your own alertness is your best hope for finding offers that reward people with your particular spending pattern.

Credit card deals change frequently. You can keep up by consulting the listings in *Kiplinger's Personal Finance* and other financial publications. For more frequent updates, consult the Kiplinger Web site (www.kiplinger.com) or those of Bank Rate Monitor (www.bankrate.com) or BanxQuote (www.banxquote.com).

Travel and Entertainment Cards

Travel and entertainment (T&E) cards, such as American Express and Diners Club, are charge cards, not credit cards. That means you are expected to pay your bill in full each month, although they may allow you to stretch out payments by establishing a line of credit with an affiliated bank. Also, American Express offers Optima, which is unabashedly a credit card and shouldn't be confused with the same company's charge card.

Membership fees for T&E cards are higher than for bank-issued cards, and the kinds of service they offer—an annual accounting of charges, traveler's checks, cash in an emergency—are commonly available with bankcards, too, especially gold cards. You may be able to get a bigger credit line with a T&E card, but they're not as widely accepted as, say, Visa or MasterCard. While there may be a resort or a store here and there that accepts these cards and excludes bankcards, you'd have to work hard to find it.

Debit Cards

A debit card appears to work the same way as a credit card: The merchant runs it through a little machine and off you go without any cash actually changing hands. But that's where the similarity ends. When you use a debit card, the amount of your purchase is deducted from your checking account or some other account you have designated. It's useful to think of a debit card as a paperless check that clears immediately, with no grace period, or "float." If you're not paying close attention, you may find yourself carrying a debit card from your bank that you think is a credit card. That mistake usually lasts no longer than the arrival of your first bank statement showing your depleted balance.

The main use for debit cards used to be to get cash from automated teller machines, but devices known as point of sale (POS) terminals have been installed in an increasing number of retail outlets. If you offer a debit card for a purchase and your balance shows up as insufficient, the terminal will disallow the transaction unless you have an overdraft credit line (see below).

Two key facts to remember about debit cards:

1. Although they look like credit cards, they aren't.

2. Safeguards against loss or theft and unauthorized use of your card aren't as strict as they are with credit cards. By law, you're liable for the same $50 as with a credit card, but only if you report an unauthorized transaction within two business days of discovering it. Miss that deadline and you're legally responsible for up to $500. But MasterCard and Visa voluntarily limit debit-card liability to $50 and will waive it entirely in many cases.

Other Lines of Instant Credit

Credit cards are convenient, but they can also be expensive. There are other sources of "instant" credit, a few of which are available at bargain rates.

Overdraft Protection

This arrangement allows you to write checks for more money than you have in your account. It's convenient in an emergency, and you avoid overdraft charges. In addition, some banks will charge overdrafts to your home equity line of credit, if you have one (see page 29), thus giving you a source of tax-deductible interest at a pretty low rate. It is one of the easiest sources of credit to use; unfortunately, it is also one of the easiest to misuse.

As with credit cards, interest rates vary among banks. Because checks cost much less to process than loan applications, banks may offer lower rates on overdraft accounts than on personal loans, especially small ones.

Because the interest on overdraft accounts is usually lower than the interest on credit card balances, these accounts can come in handy if you want to pay credit card bills in full but don't have the cash.

You can lose the interest-rate advantage if the bank imposes a transaction fee each time you write a check. Even if the fee sounds small, it can have a significant effect. Suppose your overdraft account carries a 12% APR (1% per month) and a 50-cent fee for each check. And suppose you write a $100 overdraft check and pay it back one month later. You will have paid a total charge of $1.50 for the month—the same as an APR of 18% (12 x $1.50 = $18). Whatever interest is charged, you will pay it from the date of the transaction; overdraft lines of credit don't have grace days.

Odds are that your bank will not advance you money in the exact amounts you request it. Overdraft loans are commonly made only in multiples of $50 or $100. If your bank uses the $100-multiple system, and you write a check that overdraws your account by $210, you'll have to pay interest on a $300 loan. (You will, however, have $90 left in your checking account.)

One potential drawback of overdraft credit lines is that there's often no compulsion to repay them in full right away. Some banks automatically deduct a minimum monthly payment from your checking account, but as with all minimum payments, you don't make much headway. You may find your supposedly revolving line of credit has turned into a permanent debt.

Credit Card Cash Advances

Credit card cash-advance privileges have many of the same advantages and disadvantages of overdraft accounts. Interest rates may be lower than on charges, but as a rule they're assessed from the date of the transaction, with no grace period. And a low interest rate can be, in effect, considerably higher if there's a transaction fee.

Retail Installment Credit

When you buy a big-ticket item such as furniture or a major appliance, you often have the option of paying the retailer in equal installments over a set number of months. This kind of credit may sound convenient, but it can also be expensive.

Before you sign on the dotted line, consider how the retailer's APR stacks up against what you would pay if you got a loan from a credit union, wrote a check on your overdraft account or used your credit card.

Borrowing With Collateral

Pledging collateral can help you get a bigger loan than you could get on an unsecured basis, or a break on the interest rate. Most lenders want only highly liquid assets as collateral, things that can easily be sold for cash if they must be seized to pay off the loan.

Equity in Your Home

You can tap into your home equity for fresh money by refinancing your existing first mortgage, by taking out a second mortgage or by using a home-equity line of credit.

With refinancing you negotiate a new first mortgage, use all or part of the proceeds to pay what's due on the existing loan, and pocket any difference.

If you have a low-interest loan and need to borrow more, though, it doesn't make much sense to refinance the loan. Better to keep it and borrow against your equity via a second mortgage, also called a junior mortgage. A straight second mortgage works just like a regular mortgage (see Chapter 5), although it usually lasts from five to 15 years or so rather than 25 or 30 years. These days, most second mortgages come in the form of a home-equity line of credit. Home-equity lines are available from banks, savings and loan associations and even brokerage firms. They are secured by the equity in your home, meaning the lender will foreclose if you default.

It is sometimes possible to borrow 100% of your home's appraised market value, minus what you still owe on the first mortgage, but 80% or so is a more typical limit. In many cases, there are no closing costs, but check the fine print for annual fees or other miscellaneous charges.

When you want to use a home-equity credit line, you simply write a check or use a credit card for the amount you want to borrow.

Sizing Up Home Equity Loans

Knowing the answers to these questions, adapted from a Federal Trade Commission checklist, will help you compare home-equity loans from different lenders. Before you compare, have in mind how much you want to borrow.

	Lender		
	A	B	C
What size credit line is available?			
What is the length of time for repayment?			
Is there access to loans by check or credit card?			
Is the interest rate fixed? What is it?			
Is the interest rate variable?			
What is the initial rate?			
What is the maximum rate possible?			
How often can the rate be adjusted?			
What index is used?			
What margin, if any, is added to the index?			
Can the loan be converted to a fixed rate?			
What closing costs does the borrower pay:			
Points (percent of line of credit)			
Application fee			
Title search fee			
Appraisal fee			
Attorney fee			
Other fees			
Is there an annual fee? What is it?			
Are there fees per transaction?			
What are they?			
What are the repayment terms:			
Is the monthly payment fixed?			
How much is it?			
Is the monthly payment variable?			
How much is it to begin with?			
How much is the maximum?			
Do payments cover both principal and interest?			
Are payments interest only?			
Is there a final balloon payment?			
Can a balloon be refinanced or extended?			
What's the penalty for late payments?			
What are the default provisions?			
Is there a penalty for early repayment?			

Interest generally runs one to three percentage points above the prime rate, adjusted monthly and capped at a certain level above the starting rate. You get five to ten years to repay, at which time you may have to pay the whole thing off. The main advantage of using a home-equity loan is that the interest is tax-deductible as long as the loan doesn't exceed $100,000.

Because a home-equity line of credit is, in effect, a second mortgage on your home, the application process is very similar to that for a mortgage. Use the form at left to compare the terms of loans you might consider. It shows that the best features of a particular loan aren't always obvious. You may not have to pay closing costs, for instance, but could get clobbered by lenders' fees, third-party fees and rate increases. You may discover that a low initial rate that makes one loan sound attractive is outweighed by other factors that make another loan a better bet.

How Lenders Size You Up

Imagine that you have just applied for a loan or a credit card. What's more important to your potential creditor: your income or whether you have a telephone? The age of your auto or an unblemished credit record?

The answers may surprise you. If you are being sized up by a computer rather than a loan officer, your income and credit history might count less than your having a nearly new car in the garage. Because scoring by computer is being used increasingly to decide who will get credit and who won't, you need to know how it works.

In essence, your application becomes a test, and how high you score depends on how many points you get for your answers to such questions as: How long have you been in the same job? Do you own your home or rent? How many credit cards do you have? Owning a home might be worth 15 points, for example, compared with five for renting. If you score enough points on a dozen or so questions, you get the credit; if not, you don't.

The questions that make up the test, and the score needed to pass, often depend on where you live as well as what kind of credit you want and the creditor's experience with previous customers. A computer identifies the characteristics that most clearly distinguish customers who paid their bills as agreed from those who did not, and it assigns point values to specific attributes. It then predicts the creditworthiness of applicants whose answers add up to certain scores.

One reason for the use of computer analysis as a basis for credit decisions is that the growth of credit markets to include nationwide retailers and credit card issuers has made it comparatively rare for a lender to know applicants or their references personally. With the loss of such firsthand information, the methods of winnowing out bad credit risks have grown impersonal.

But there's another reason lenders are leaning on computers to make their decisions. Federal law limits the criteria that can be used to decide who will get credit. The Equal Credit Opportunity Act prohibits discrimination on a number of grounds. A lender can program a computer to consider only legally permissible information and to apply the same standards to all applicants.

This doesn't mean that all credit scoring systems use the same criteria. A trait that's valuable in one system may carry little weight in another. A doctor might win high points for his profession from a bank but very few from a finance company, which might wonder why such a high-income individual would show up at its door.

Although the way you've handled credit in the past—your credit record—is considered by most lenders to be the best predictor of your future performance, it might not be scored. Many creditors check with a credit bureau only if a score falls in a gray area between automatic approval and automatic rejection. When it is considered, a bad credit record—several late payments, for instance—can knock down an otherwise passing grade. A good record might boost your score to the approval level.

If You Are Denied Credit

What if you are denied credit? If a credit report helped tip the scales against you, you must be told the name of the bureau that provided the information so you have an opportunity to find out whether outdated or erroneous data killed the deal. If you're turned down for credit, take the time to find out what the credit bureau is saying about you. The federal Fair Credit Reporting Act arms you with the following weapons:

- **You have the right to receive a copy** of your report at no charge if you've been denied credit within the past 60 days. Otherwise, you can be charged a modest fee. (See the phone numbers of the national credit-reporting agencies on page 20.)

Other Laws That Protect Your Rights

When you apply for and use credit, you should expect a fair deal from the lender. In addition to the Fair Credit Reporting Act, three other federal laws protect your rights: the Truth in Lending Act, the Equal Credit Opportunity Act, and the Fair Credit Billing Act. You could benefit from detailed knowledge of these laws, but we'll just highlight them here.

The Truth in Lending Act

Federal truth-in-lending rules require that lenders express the cost of borrowing as the annual percentage rate, or APR. This piece of information, which allows you to compare like quantities, is essential for shopping the cost of loans. The APR and the method of calculating the finance charge must appear prominently on lenders' loan disclosure forms; otherwise, they are not in compliance with truth-in-lending rules.

The Equal Credit Opportunity Act

This law says that you cannot be denied credit because of sex, marital status, age, race, color, religion, national origin, your receipt of public-assistance income, or your exercise of your rights under truth-in-lending and other credit laws. Neither this law nor any other guarantees credit. There are many valid reasons for a creditor to deny credit. But the law guarantees that your creditworthiness will be evaluated on the same basis as that of all other customers. The law contains a number of special provisions designed to protect women.

The Fair Credit Billing Act

The heart of the Fair Credit Billing Act obligates credit card issuers and firms that extend revolving-type credit to do the following:

- **Credit payments to your account** the day the payments are received at the address the company has specified.

- **Mail your bill at least** 14 days before payment is due, if your account is the type that gives you a period of time to pay before finance charges are assessed.

- **Send you a detailed explanation** of your rights and remedies under this law twice a year or enclose a brief explanation with every bill and send the longer explanation when you ask for it.

- **Follow certain procedures** in resolving complaints you may make about billing errors.

- **You have the right to expect the credit bureau to investigate** any errors that you report, and to recontact the creditor who reported the negative information.
- **If the creditor involved confirms the information** but you still think it's wrong, you have the right to add a short statement to your file, telling your side of the story.

What to Do

Call the credit bureau to have your report mailed to you and arrange an appointment to review your file.

Federal law requires that most unfavorable reports be purged after seven years (ten in the case of bankruptcy) so that past financial problems won't haunt someone for life. Creditors are generally most interested in the past couple of years.

If you find incorrect information in your credit record, demand that the credit bureau investigate the report. If it can't verify the accuracy of the item, the information must be dropped from your file. When unfavorable information is accurate, you may be able to minimize its damage by attaching to the report a short statement. If you missed several payments during a period in which you were unemployed or ill, for example, an explanation of the extenuating circumstances might give you a better chance with the next potential creditor who calls up your report.

Assuming your report is changed after your review, either because negative information is dropped or because an explanation is attached, you can have the credit bureau send the revised report to credit grantors who got the original version during the previous six months.

Chapter 3

Protecting Your Life

First, a word about insurance in general. You need insurance for two reasons: one, to protect you and your family from the consequences of a financial loss—affecting your health, your car, your home, your belongings or your life—and two, to make good on your obligations to others who might suffer injury or loss for which you are responsible.

What you get for your money is a promise to pay if the event you hope never happens *does* happen. In most cases, if the dreaded event doesn't happen, about the only tangible thing you have to show for your money is the policy document itself and maybe a card you carry in your wallet. You may also have a stack of canceled checks, a reminder of what a big ticket item insurance can be. This section covers life insurance; homeowners and car insurance are covered elsewhere in the guidebook.

What Have You Got?

An insurance policy is a legal contract, with specific meanings attached to certain words. Those words spell out your rights and obligations as well as those of the insurance company. Unless your policy expressly calls for the payment of a certain benefit upon the occurrence of a certain event, you probably won't be paid, no matter what a salesperson or other representative may have told you. If the fine print takes away what the big print appears to bestow, that's your tough luck. What's more, the marketplace is constantly in flux, characterized by increasingly complex policies, changes in coverage, wildly varying rates, confusing discounts. A lot of smart people work for insurance companies, and they are always thinking up new policies with new twists. As mind-numbing as it sounds, there's really only one way to know what's in your policies: Read them, each and every one, new or renewal, from front to back, with a dictionary at your elbow and perhaps the phone numbers of your agents at hand. Understand what's behind the policy titles, which are only occasionally informative. What would you know from their titles about life insurance policies named Contender, Vision, Preference or Optimiser 100? Some insurance companies have undertaken laudable campaigns to make their policies more understandable. But don't get your hopes up: There's still a long way to go.

When Should You Buy Life Insurance?

Your need for life insurance changes with the stages of your life, starting with no need when you're young, progressing to greater and greater need as you take on more and more responsibility, and finally beginning to diminish as you grow older. Consider these situations:

When You're Single
Sad though your death would be, it would create financial hardship for no one. Any honest financial assessment of your situation would have to conclude that you have little or no need for life insurance. An argument could be made that you should buy a policy now while you're young and rates are low. And if someone—a parent, say—depends on you for financial support, then by all means consider life insurance. But consider the interest you could earn by saving and investing your money instead of spending it on insurance premiums.

Love and Marriage
A few years have gone by and now you're half of a married couple with no children. Together you earn $70,000 a year, each contributing about equally. The death of either of you would not be financially catastrophic; the other could presumably survive on his or her own income. Still, it could be a strain. Perhaps the survivor couldn't afford the mortgage or rent payments on a single income, or maybe you have big credit card debts. Also, there would be funeral costs. Each of you should probably buy a modest amount of life insurance to protect the other.

Married With Children
More time passes. Now you're half of a couple living in a one-income household. You have two young children. This is the classic high-need situation. Four people are dependent on one breadwinner for their total support, so insurance on that life is vital. And if the non-earning spouse should die, the other would have to pay for child care—a very expensive proposition that argues for insurance on both lives. This same high-need situation exists for dual-income households with children, for single parents, and for anyone caring for elderly parents who have limited resources of their own.

The Golden Years
Now you're retired. The kids have grown and are making it on their own. You have a pension and considerable assets that can be used to generate a good income after you die. In circumstances like this, you clearly don't need as much life insurance as you once did. Still, life insurance can come in handy for estate planning.

How Much Do You Need?

Deciding whether you need life insurance is pretty easy. Figuring out how much you need is not easy at all. Many people just pluck some figure out of the air that seems reasonable and settle on that. Some lean on an old rule of thumb that says you need four to five times your annual income. That's better, but in this day and age you really should approach the problem more scientifically. You can arrive at a reasonable estimate of your life insurance needs without getting too technical, and the worksheet on page 39 will help you do it.

The first step is to estimate the income your dependents would need to maintain their standard of living if you were to die tomorrow. Then subtract from that figure the income they could expect to receive in social security survivor's benefits (to get the form you need to estimate that, call the Social Security Administration at 800–772–1213 or visit the agency's Web site at www.ssa.gov). Next subtract the salaries your dependents now earn or could earn, the value of investments and other income sources. The difference is the amount of income your life insurance should provide.

You have to make a number of assumptions in the course of this exercise—complex assumptions that scare many people away from the task. For instance:

- **What will inflation be in the future?** Unless you've got some special insight into this question, assume that it will average 4%.
- **Will the family be able to live on the earnings** generated by the proceeds of the policy, or should they expect to gradually use up the capital as well? The answer to this depends a great deal on how much money is involved. If the policy will pay a half-million dollars and there are other sources of income, then you can reasonably expect that the beneficiaries could use the earnings and leave the principal pretty much alone. On the other hand, if the policy pays $100,000, then the family will need considerable additional assets if the principal is to remain intact.
- **What rate of interest** can you safely assume the money will earn? For a conservative after-tax return based on historical norms, you should assume 8%.
- **Will your spouse take a jo**b if he or she doesn't have one now? Will that require a period of training? How much can your spouse realistically be expected to earn? The answers will depend on your own situation, of course. It is impossible to anticipate everything, but it's wise to make reasonable guesses about what sorts of choices the surviving spouse might confront and provide as much breathing room as you can afford.

You can see what makes this task so difficult. Insurance companies will make the financial assumptions for you, using computerized programs developed for the purpose. These can be helpful, but many of the decisions described above are too important to turn over completely to the company trying to sell you the policy.

Eventually you will have to pick some total insurance figure that seems a reasonable compromise between what you'd like to have and what you can afford, using the companies' estimates for reference. Keep in mind that the purchasing power of the insurance you buy today will be eroded by inflation as the years go by. Remember the inflation assumption you made above and refer to the inflation table on page 145 to get an idea of the effect of that on your coverage five or ten years down the road.

The Life Insurance Menu

Life insurance companies are brilliant at devising new kinds of policies. But try to remember that whatever the name on the policy—

Figuring Your Life Insurance Needs

A. Survivors' Annual Expenses
Annual expenditures from Cash-flow worksheet
(see Chapter 1, page 7)
Minus your own living expenses   − _____
                A. Total annual expenses $ _____

B. Survivors' Annual Income
Anticipated salaries   _____
Interest from savings   _____
Investment dividends   _____
Rents received   _____
Annuity income   _____
Social security benefits   _____
Veterans benefits   _____
Payments from pension plan   _____
Income from trusts   _____
Other income   +   _____
             B. Total annual income available $ _____

C. Annual Income Needed From Additional Insurance
Annual expenses minus annual
income (A minus B)   _____
Minus annual benefits from
existing life insurance policies   −   _____

Annual income needed from additional insurance $ _____

---

universal life, variable life, Irresistible Life, Irreplaceable Life, The Champion, The Solution—all are in fact variations on the two basic kinds of coverage: term insurance and cash-value insurance (also called permanent or whole life).

Term Insurance

This is as simple as life insurance gets and is the easiest to understand. You insure your life for a certain amount of money for a fixed period of time—one year, five years or more—and pay an annual premium based on your age and the amount of coverage you're buying. There's nothing fancy about term insurance. It has no savings or investment features built into the rates, making it the purest form of life insurance around and thus the cheapest for a given amount of coverage.

Annual-renewable term
You buy a series of one-year policies and the insurance company guarantees you the right to renew the coverage each year without having to undergo an additional medical exam. Your premium rises with each new policy year.

Guaranteed-level term
Instead of rising each year, premiums start out a little higher but stay level for five, ten, 15 or even 20 years or more. At the end of the period, you have usually paid less than you would have under an annual-renewable term policy. Insurance companies developed guaranteed-level term policies to discourage customers from hopping from one company to another each year at policy renewal time, chasing the lowest rates.

Declining, decreasing or reducing term
The amount of coverage gradually declines according to a fixed schedule over ten, 15, 20 or more years. Mortgage insurance policies, which pay the loan balance when the policyholder dies, are a common form of decreasing term.

Convertible term
For a higher premium than regular term, a convertible policy can be rolled into a whole life, or cash-value policy without your having to meet medical standards at the time of conversion. Most companies offer policies that are both convertible and renewable up to specified ages or for fixed periods.

Whole-Life Insurance
This is commonly called cash-value or permanent insurance. In its basic form, it charges you the same premium for as long as you keep the policy. Because the premium remains level as you grow older, it must be set to exceed the company's cost of insuring your life during the early years. The extra premium and the interest it earns go into a reserve fund. Part of the fund is used to pay the agent's commission and the company's administrative costs. The rest gets credited to your account, where it earns interest. After a couple of years your reserve begins to build, tax free, creating a "cash value" that you can draw on in a number of ways.

You can get at your accumulated cash value by borrowing against it while the policy stays in force; by directing the company to use it to purchase a paid-up insurance policy of some amount; by directing the company to use it to pay your premiums; or by surrendering the policy and taking the money. When you die, if the policy is still in force, the company pays your beneficiary the policy's face amount (less any loan balance), *not* the face amount plus cash value.

Insurance companies offer a wondrous array of cash-value policies, ranging from the standard, no-frills kind (sometimes called straight or ordinary life) to specially designed contracts in which the premiums or face amounts change according to a set schedule, investment results or some other factor.

Even though some of the excess premiums charged by whole-life insurance policies in their early years may eventually find their way into your pocket via the cash-value buildup, the question remains: Why give all that extra money to the insurance company when you could simply buy term insurance and invest the difference yourself? This is the great debate of the ages in the insurance industry.

Making Sure the Right People Collect

Most people don't run into beneficiary difficulties with their life insurance, perhaps because their lives generally follow the anticipated course. A husband designates his wife as beneficiary; he dies; she receives the money as he intended. However, you can't be sure that even well-conceived beneficiary arrangements won't be upset by later events. To avoid problems, get familiar with these essential points.

Naming Beneficiaries

A policy owner can name anyone he or she chooses as beneficiary—relative, friend, business associate, charity. You can also change beneficiaries unless you have previously named someone as the irrevocable beneficiary. In that case you must obtain the beneficiary's permission. Irrevocable designations result most often from divorce and separation settlements. Beneficiaries can be changed merely by filling out a company form and sending it to the company.

If you die without having recorded a living beneficiary with the company, the proceeds will be paid into your estate or sometimes to surviving children, depending on the terms of the policy.

Designating your beneficiaries

The normal procedure is to name a primary beneficiary and a secondary, or contingent, beneficiary in case the primary should die before you do. You can even select a third beneficiary to receive the money in the event neither the primary nor secondary beneficiary survives you.

If you name two or more beneficiaries of equal rank, the funds will be divided equally unless you provide otherwise. Two primary beneficiaries, for example, would receive 50% each.

Leaving it to your spouse

To avoid confusion, a wife or husband should be identified by his or her given name. Mrs. John Nelson, for example, should be described as "Mrs. Jane Nelson" or "Jane Nelson, wife of the insured." For further specification, her premarital surname could be added—for example, "Mrs. Jane Smith Nelson." If a woman has kept her premarital surname, then of course the policy should use it.

Leaving it to the kids

"My children" or "children of the insured" or some similar collective designation usually suffices because it usually covers all present and future children, including adopted children. However, a broad description might have to be modified to cope with a specific situation, such as stepchildren.

Leaving it to a minor

When you name a child as beneficiary, legal problems may arise if the proceeds of your insurance have to be paid while he or she is still a minor. To protect itself against future claims, the insurance company will want a valid receipt for payments, and a minor may not be considered legally qualified for that purpose. State laws vary considerably, but in some cases the court may decide to appoint a guardian to receive and take care of the funds.

To avoid those difficulties, appoint a trustee to accept the insurance money and administer it for the child's benefit while he or she is a minor. The trustee could be directed in the trust agreement to pay the child any funds remaining at the time the child reaches his or her majority. You can also appoint a successor trustee to take over if the first becomes unable to serve.

Working the Tax Angles
The beneficiary of a life insurance policy gets three big tax breaks:
- **No income tax** has to be paid on the money.

- **The funds don't have to go through** the often time-consuming and possibly expensive probate procedures required for assets that are transferred by a will.

- **The state may exempt** part or all of the money from its estate tax or inheritance tax.

Life insurance proceeds may not be completely tax-free because the money is included in the estate of the policy owner when *federal* estate taxes are figured. But it's possible to move life insurance out of your estate by making the beneficiary of the policy the owner of the policy. That means you give up the right to the cash value and the right to change the beneficiary. You could also transfer ownership of the policy to an irrevocable living trust, whose terms normally can't be changed.

By taking either of these steps, you in effect make a gift of the insurance to someone else and may have to pay a gift tax. If you think you need estate-tax planning, don't try doing it on your own with ready-made forms. Consult an experienced estate-planning attorney.

Picking the Payoff Method

Life insurance proceeds are usually paid out in a lump sum. But insurance companies also offer several alternative arrangements. As a policy owner, you can select one of these settlement options for your beneficiary. If you make no choice, the beneficiary can elect one within a certain period after your death. These are the options commonly available:

Interest Only
The funds are left on deposit with the insurance company, which guarantees a minimum rate of interest but normally pays more. Interest is paid to the beneficiary, who can be given the right to withdraw principal as desired.

Installments for a Fixed Period
The proceeds are paid out in equal amounts for as long as the money lasts. Again, the company usually adds extra interest to its guaranteed rate.

Shop from Home for Life Insurance

One of the most convenient ways to get comparative quotes on term insurance is to use one of the national quote services. They are, in effect, insurance agents, meaning they are paid commissions by the companies they represent. To improve your chances of finding the lowest premiums for the coverage you want, check with at least two national quote services and an independent agent before making your choice. The listings show toll-free numbers and, when they exist, addresses for Web sites.

Term Policies
InstantQuote   www.instantquote.com
888–223–2220
MasterQuote   www.masterquote.com
800–337–5433
LifeRates of America
800–457–2837
TermQuote   www.termquote.com
800–444–8376
Quotesmith   www.quotesmith.com
800–556–9393
QuickQuote   www.quickquote.com
800–867–2404
SelectQuote   www.selectquote.com
800–343–1985
ConsumerQuote USA   www.consumerquote.com
800–552–7283
InsuranceQuote Services   www.iquote.com
800–972–1104
Quicken InsureMarket   www.quicken.com/insurance

Cash-Value Policies
In shopping for whole-life insurance, it's a good idea to check with financial planners and insurance agents. A few companies sell directly to the public or through fee-only planners.

Veritas   www.veritas.ameritas.com
800–555–4655
USAA
800–531–4440

Life Income
The beneficiary is guaranteed a lifetime income based on his or her age and on the amount of the proceeds. The company may allow the beneficiary to use the proceeds to buy one of its regular annuities at a discount.

Which should you choose? Consider installment and annuity plans if you're protecting a beneficiary who doesn't have the experience to manage a large sum. But be aware that a beneficiary can often invest the money safely at a better rate than the insurance company offers. In most cases, you should leave the choice of a settlement option to the beneficiary.

Chapter 4

How to Have Investing Smarts

You want your own home, an education for your kids, a comfortable retirement and some fun along the way. These are the standard-issue dreams we all have. To achieve them, we must become investors. Saving up for things is a good habit to cultivate for a lifetime, but saving up isn't enough because you can't possibly earn enough interest to get you where you want to go.

A brilliantly executed program of saving—putting your money into certificates of deposit, money-market funds or savings bonds—is capable of earning 5% to 6% in a good year. Consider that 3% or so is a reasonable expectation for inflation (some would say that's optimistic) and that taxes will nick 28% or so of what remains, and you can see what you're up against: 5% quickly becomes about 1.4% after inflation and taxes. You're going to have to do a lot better than that.

To drive the lesson home: Suppose you start with $1,000 in a CD earning 5% compounded daily and set aside $250 a month for a new certificate earning the same. Continue for ten years and you'll have a little more than $41,000, before taxes. In 20 years you'll have about $107,000 (compounding makes the 20-year return more than twice the ten-year return).

Not too shabby, but it won't buy you that condo on the golf course, especially at prices twenty years down the road, plus pay for college in the interim. To increase your return, you must become an investor, not just a saver, which means taking some risks.

Investing seemed like a pretty sure thing in the '90s, when the stock market was regularly piling up returns of 20% and more. Elated investors congratulated each other on their genius. But let's face it: You don't have to be a genius to make money in such markets. You don't even have to pay very close attention to what you're doing. And if the market could pound out returns like that indefinitely, you could put all your money in an index fund and throw away this guidebook.

Alas, it doesn't work that way. There is no endless summer; you need an investment plan for all seasons. Stocks should be a big part of it, but you can choose from an overwhelming number of other options. Interest rates, inflation, corporate profits, and consumer and investor psychology affect the prospects for different investments in different ways at different times. And brokerage firms, banks, insurance companies and others are ingenious at devising new investment products that let you take advantage of the changes.

How much more will you need to earn than you could get through saving alone? You should aim for an annual return of 10% to 12% per year on your investments. That's an achievable range if you plan your approach thoughtfully and stick to your plan.

You're Going to Need a Plan

Successful investors don't jump from one place to another according to what's hot and what's not. They have a plan that's based on their goals, how long they have to achieve them, their tolerance for risk (both financial and psychological), and what they can afford to set aside for an investment program. You want to make money, of course, but you also want to be able to sleep at night. Here's how to do it.

Set Exciting Goals
Chapter 1 described the importance of short-term goal setting when drawing up a budget for the year ahead. Investment goals tend to be long-term: enough to pay college tuition starting in ten years, for instance, or enough to retire on in 15 or 20 years. It's this long-range outlook that causes many people to set such vague, halfhearted goals that they can't maintain the discipline necessary to reach them.

If you set merely "retirement" as a goal, what will motivate you to get there (besides the relentless passage of time)? To build motivation into your goal-setting, go a few steps further: Where would you like to live when you retire? How much will it cost? What would you like to do? Travel? Sail the Caribbean? How much income will you need in addition to your pension? This kind of thinking lets you add flesh to your bare-bones goal to "retire someday." How about this: "Our goal is to retire at age 58 to a three-bedroom house near the Grand Canyon in Arizona, with room for the grandkids who will come to visit. We want to travel at least two months of the year in the U.S. and Europe, and we'll need $2,000 a month to supplement our pensions." Now you've got goals you can pin a price tag on, and a nice mental picture to remind you of why you're pouring all that money into delayed gratification.

Adopt a Clear-Cut Strategy

Brokerage firms, mutual funds and the daily financial press produce lots of useful information for investors. But you don't have to read very much of it before you realize how contradictory it can be. The developments used to explain yesterday's drop in stocks may be the same ones cited for today's rise. One expert recommends buying utility stocks and selling computer stocks, while another advises us to sell utilities and buy computers. No *wonder* we're confused.

View this day-to-day crystal-ball gazing with clear-eyed vision and create your own strategy based on your own goals, risk tolerance and psychological makeup. For example, three different investors might devise strategies like the following.

- **Sticking with stocks.** "Stocks offer the best returns over the long run. I have more than a decade to ride out any market dips, so I'm going to play the averages and put 90% of my money in the stock market. The rest I'll keep in savings, insured certificates of deposit and money-market funds."

- **Rooted in real estate.** "I think that rental real estate, despite its occasional setbacks, offers the best chance of long-term gain and steady income. I know the local market well, and I'll try to keep 40% of my assets in real estate and diversify the rest, putting some in the money market for liquidity and some in big-company stocks to balance the risks in real estate."

- **Spreading the risks.** "I don't have a clue what's going on in the investment markets and I don't have the time to keep up with them, so I'll spread my money across a wide range of investments in the hope that gains in some categories will offset losses in others. I will invest 60% in stock-oriented mutual funds, 20% in corporate bonds, 10% in money-market funds and CDs, and 10% in shares of a real estate investment trust."

These are made-up scenarios, of course. Your own plan may

look nothing like them, but you should go through the thought process so that investment decisions you make will be guided by your own strategy, not that of a broker or adviser trying to sell you something. A successful strategy can probably be summarized in three or four sentences, just like the ones above.

Pay Attention

As time passes, investment plans take on lives of their own. Interest rates rise and fall. Big-company stocks pass in and out of favor. Real estate markets plunge and soar. To make sure your investment plan is still on track, sit down once a year or so and update the values of what you own, including the equity in your home. Compute each type of investment—stocks, bonds, mutual funds and so forth—as a percentage of the total. If you haven't achieved an asset mix you like, this exercise will show you which parts must be increased, and which cut back. As the years go by, the percentage mix of your investments will change without your lifting a finger, as some parts of your portfolio rise in value and others fall. This makes a periodic review imperative. Money-management software makes it a snap.

Control Your Risks

The risks you're prepared to take will influence the kinds of investments you make and the expected return. These four rules will keep you in a comfortable risk zone. (And again, let you sleep at night.)

1. **Don't invest until you're ready to invest.** Your investment portfolio should be built on a solid foundation of sure things: sufficient insurance coverage and several months' income tucked securely away in an interest-bearing bank account or money-market fund. Only when you have that cushion are you ready to start investing.

2. **Invest aggressively for the long term and conservatively for the short term.** This means that stocks should be thought of as investments for achieving long-term goals. For short-term goals—money you'll need within a few years—stick with CDs and other sure bets.

3. **Don't invest very much money in anything that still leaves you uneasy after you have investigated its strengths and weaknesses.** The bigger the promised reward, the bigger your risk. This doesn't mean you should never take big risks; just don't take big risks with big chunks of your money.

4. **Don't buy anything you don't know how to sell.** Some so-called investments, such as collectibles and gemstones, are simple to buy but may take specialized assistance to sell because there are no organized national resale markets, as there are for stocks and bonds.

Make Investing a Habit

Dollar-cost averaging is a reliable way to smooth out the ups and downs of the stock market. It works like this: You invest a fixed amount on a regular schedule, ignoring the prices at the time. The amount can be $25 a month, $50 a month, $500 a month—whatever fits your budget. Your fixed number of dollars automatically buys more shares when prices are low than when prices are high. As a result, the average purchase price of your stock will be lower than the average of the market prices over the same length of time.

Dollar-cost averaging won't automatically produce a profit. But by investing on a regular schedule and sticking with it, you're almost guaranteed to do better in a generally rising market, with the usual ups and downs, than investors who try to sell at the top and buy at the bottom. Historically, the odds are strongly against that kind of timing.

How can you buy small amounts of stock on a regular basis without going broke paying the commissions?

First, a growing number of companies will sell shares directly to investors, allowing you to bypass brokers' commissions. These programs also make you eligible for the company's dividend reinvestment plan, or DRIP. For a list of companies offering such plans, check *TheMoneypaper* (phone 800–388–9993, or check the Web site at www.directinvesting.com/moneypaper) or Netstock Direct (888–638–7865 or www.netstockdirect.com).

Second, no-load mutual funds are ideally suited for dollar-cost averaging. There are no sales commissions when you buy, and you can invest a small (or large) amount of money on a regular schedule, even if your dollars buy fractional shares. Many funds will let you have money transferred regularly from a bank account, thus creating for you an enforced investment plan that will grow as the years go by.

Don't Get Stuck in a Rut

The time may come when you want to revise your strategy. Retirement, for instance, may be a time to lighten up a bit (but not entirely) on stocks and emphasize income-oriented investments such as bonds.

Try to avoid abrupt changes in direction, and *don't* try to time the market. You can change your asset mix gradually by allocating new investment money from savings, dividends and interest to the category you want to increase.

Don't Fool Yourself
Investment expectations are easy to exaggerate by fixating on an investment's most favorable period—the stock market in the 1990s, for instance, or real estate markets in the 1970s. On average, a total return of 10% to 15% per year on your investments—that is, the sum of dividends and interest plus price increases of your holdings—is a reasonable, achievable expectation. Some years you'll do better, others worse.

You'll have ups and downs, so keep in mind the trade-off between risk and reward. A conservative investor sacrifices potential gain in order to limit potential losses. An aggressive investor sacrifices safety in hopes of a bigger gain.

How Not to Get Ripped Off

There's hardly a legitimate investment that isn't considered fair game by crooks. They sell low-priced stocks, precious metals, rare coins, commodity contracts, diamonds, real estate—you name it and someone will find a way to make a scam out of it.

Investment rackets often originate in telephone "boiler rooms," where squads of high-pressure salespeople canvass the nation with get-rich-quick schemes. Sometimes the approach is low-key; sometimes it's so pressure-packed that usually-sensible people get rattled into parting with their money. The message is the same: You can make a lot of money by taking advantage of the rare opportunity you're being offered, and you'd better move fast.

Some scams are so comical that it's hard to believe anyone would fall for them (and we'd like to think *we* wouldn't). But people have been sold shares in companies claiming to be developing underwater home sites, or pelts from giant rabbits. The crooks are often so clever, talking jargon and spinning out scenarios so fast, that their victims aren't sure what's happening. To guard against this, approach any unfamiliar investment with the following rules firmly in mind.

•**Deal Only With Established Businesses**

- Don't Fall for Inflated Promises
- Don't Buy What You Don't Understand
- Check Out the Seller

    Contact the appropriate organization to see if complaints have been filed against the firm you're dealing with.

    Stockbrokers and mutual funds: National Association of Securities Dealers (800–289–9999 or www.nasd.com) and ask for the Central Registration Depository report (CRD) on the broker. For a more detailed report, call the securities regulation office of the state in which the broker operates.

    Business opportunities: Federal Trade Commission, CRC-240, Washington, DC 20580 (877-382-4357 or www.ftc.gov). But be aware that the FTC will not tell you about complaints unless it has acted on them.

    Land sales: Interstate Land Sales Registration, U.S. Department of Housing and Urban Development, 451 Seventh St., S.W., Washington, DC 20410 (www.hud.gov).

    Commodities contracts: Commodity Futures Trading Commission, Office of Public Affairs, Three Lafayette Center, 1155 21st St., N.W., Washington, DC 20581(www.cftc.gov); or National Futures Association, which has a toll-free number, 800–621–3570 (in Illinois, call 800–572–9400) and a Web site (www.nfa.futures.org).

    Anything that comes in the mail: U.S. Postal Service, Chief Postal Inspector, 475 L'Enfant Plaza, S.W., Washington, DC 20060–0010 (www.usps.gov), or contact the postal inspector in your area.

If you get suspicious, get out fast. Stop payment on your check. Demand your money back. Threaten to go to the authorities. A crook doesn't want their attention, so this sort of fuss works more often than you might think. If you think you're being ripped off, holler.

Hiring Help: How to Pick a Financial Planner

Investment markets change fast and it's hard to keep up. Plus, it's not always easy to be objective about your own financial situation and decide on the proper mix of insurance and investments. A good stockbroker can help, but if you'd like someone to make broader investment recommendations based on extensive knowledge of your financial situation, you may be in the market for a financial planner. Candidates aren't hard to find; just look in your local Yellow Pages. You can also get names of planners in your area from the profession's major membership organizations listed on page 54.

Select at least three candidates. Visit their offices and ask for detailed statements of fees and services, resumes and references. Then compare them on the following points.

Experience

Financial planning is a wide and varied field, and not everyone in it matches the popular image of the sage, seasoned counselor. However, your planner should have, at the very least, a few years of experience in planning or allied fields, such as accounting, securities analysis or trading, or law.

Credentials

Many practitioners have pulled themselves above the crowd by taking courses and passing exams that lead to a professional designation.

Certified Financial Planner (CFP) is probably the best-known credential. Graduates must take a series of courses, pass a two-day, 10-hour exam and complete three years of work experience to earn the CFP designation. The coursework usually takes several years to complete, and the planner must also complete 30 hours of continuing education every two years.

Chartered Financial Consultants (ChFC) have earned the designation from the American College in Bryn Mawr, Pa., which also grants an insurance-business certification, Chartered Life Underwriter. The ChFC has successfully completed a an eight-course sequence over a period of two to four years and passed two-hour exams on each.

Master of Sciences in Financial Services (MSFS) is also conferred by the American College, after 36 credits of coursework and two weeks of study at the college.

Registered Financial Consultants (RFC) meet the requirements of the International Association of Registered Financial Planners, which confers the designation on planners who meet certain academic and work-experience guidelines.

These titles do provide some assurance that the planner took the trouble to take the courses to raise his or her level of skill and knowledge in the field.

Access to Experts
No one person, however well trained, has the encyclopedic knowledge required to deal in depth with all the problems that can affect an individual's financial affairs. That would require knowing as

---

How to Find a Qualified Financial Planner

• **For a directory** of fee-only practitioners, contact the National Association of Personal Financial Advisors, 355 W. Dundee Road, Suite 200, Buffalo Grove, IL 60089; www.napfa.org or 800–366–2732.

• **For names of CPAs** who have earned the credential of Accredited Personal Financial Specialist, contact the American Institute of CPAs, Personal Financial Planning Division, 1211 Avenue of the Americas, New York, NY 10036; 212–596–6200 or 888-777-7077.

• **The Financial Planning Association** has a registry service you can use to get names of members in your area. Contact them at 404–845–0011 or 800-282-PLAN or visit their website at www.fpanet.org.

---

much about, say, estate planning and insurance as commodity futures. Instead, a planner should be able to demonstrate that he or she consults regularly with experts in a variety of fields.

Fees and Commissions
There's no standard fee system or scale in the planning business. At one end of the spectrum are planners who work only for fees, much like lawyers. At the other end are firms that operate entirely or almost entirely on commissions. In between are those who depend on a combination of fees and commissions. In some cases the planner might partly credit commissions against the fee to encourage

the client to buy insurance or other financial products through the planner's company.

A planner who feels confident of being able to sell a high-commission product might gamble on a low fee. Assume, for instance, you're charged $1,000 for a complete plan plus a certain number of hours of interviews and consultation time. If you put $20,000 in a mutual fund with a 5% sales charge, or load, your planner would make $1,000, and only $19,000 would buy shares in the fund.

Unless you're dealing with a fee-only firm, you can expect to get suggestions that you purchase an investment or insurance product that the planner sells. There's nothing wrong with that, provided the product is suitable for someone in your financial situation and compares favorably with the scores of others you might buy elsewhere.

If the product is insurance, for example, and the policy is right for you and competitively priced, you might as well buy it from the planner. But your attitude should be different about mutual funds and securities. You'd want to think twice about buying a load fund when there are so many no-load funds available, for instance. And why buy the stocks recommended by the planner at a standard commission rate when you can use a discount broker? It's up to you to decide whether the quality of the planner's service is worth the cost.

Chapter 5

Buying a Home

Homeownership is an enduring part of the American dream, not to mention the American way of life. Six out of ten American households own the roof over their heads, and three of the other four aspire to own it. Homeownership is considered a sign of maturity, stability and financial independence. It can even be the path to some profit.

This chapter will make the case for homeownership, describe the different forms it can take, suggest ways to make your home-buying experience a happy one, and go into the details of getting a mortgage.

There are three compelling reasons to own your home.

You Get a Tax Shelter Unmatched Anywhere Else

It may not be fair to renters, but the tax laws favor homeowners—no question about it. If you rent, you pay the owner's mortgage interest and property taxes as part of your rent, but only the owner gets to deduct them from taxable income. Fortunately, you don't have to be a landlord to claim these write-offs. All you have to do is own the place.

In the early years of a mortgage, nearly all of your monthly payments go toward fully deductible interest. Take a conventional, 30-year, $100,000 mortgage at a fixed rate of 8%. Each year interest and principal payments total $8,805. In the first year $7,970 of that amount—more than 90% of it—is deductible as interest. Even in the 15th year, about 70% of your monthly payments would be deductible.

Interest on up to $1 million of mortgage debt is fully deductible. What this is worth to you depends on your tax bracket. Let's say you're in the 28% federal tax bracket. That's an income between about $26,250 and $63,550 if you're single, or about $43,850 and $105,950 if you file a joint return. In the 28% bracket, $1,000 in deductions saves you $280 in taxes. So, for each $1,000 of housing payments consisting of interest and property taxes, Uncle Sam pays $280 by reducing your federal income-tax bill by that amount. You save some on top of that by taking the same deductions on your state income-tax return.

When you sell the place, you can make a profit of up to $250,000 ($500,000 for a couple) without owing a dime of tax on the gain. There is absolutely no other way to make that kind of money and legally get to keep it all.

Homeowners can also use the equity in their home as a source of tax-sheltered loans. You can borrow against your home (through either a second mortgage or a home-equity line of credit) and deduct all the interest you pay on up to $100,000 of such loans, regardless of how you use the money. (For more information, see Chapter 2.)

What Do You Want in a Home?

Price range: _____

Desired neighborhoods:
_____
_____
_____

Desired school districts:
_____
_____
_____

How far are you willing to commute?
_____

Would you prefer:
❏ an older home
❏ a new home

Architectural style of home:
❏ one-story ❏ two-story
❏ split-level
❏ colonial ❏ contemporary
❏ other: _____

Are you willing to take on a fixer-upper?
❏ yes ❏ no

Number of bedrooms you need: ___
Number of bathrooms: ___

Master bedroom suite? ❏ yes ❏ no

Check off the features that you want in a home:

Very Important	Negotiable	
❏	❏	Public transportation nearby
❏	❏	Yard
❏	❏	Eat-in kitchen
❏	❏	Fireplace
❏	❏	Separate dining room
❏	❏	Walk-in closets
❏	❏	Finished basement
❏	❏	Walk-out basement
❏	❏	Garage
❏	❏	Expandability
❏	❏	Located on a cul-de-sac
❏	❏	Plenty of windows and light
❏	❏	Family neighborhood
❏	❏	Close to shopping

Other features you want (list):
_____
_____
_____
_____

You Join the Leverage Club

Most people buy a home with a little bit of their own money and a lot of somebody else's. This use of borrowed money means you can profit from price increases on property you haven't even paid for yet. That's the "leverage" everybody talks about. The bigger your loan as a proportion of the home's value, the greater your leverage. Say you buy a home for $100,000 with no mortgage and sell it three years later for $110,000. The $10,000 gain represents a 10% return on your $100,000 outlay after three years. That's okay, but not great.

Now look at the deal another way: Make a down payment of $20,000 and get a mortgage for the rest. You still make a $10,000 profit after three years of ownership, but you've invested only $20,000 to get it. Your return: a spectacular 50% on your investment (ignoring for the sake of simplicity the cost of the loan, tax angles, commissions and other costs).

You Get a Hedge Against Inflation

People aren't worried much about inflation these days, but what if it were to heat up? What would happen to home prices? Well, let's look to the past for a clue. In the high-inflation period from the mid 1970s to the early 1980s, the cost of living rose about 70%. Home prices doubled in the same period. Since then, in a time of generally tame inflation, home values in general have risen a little faster than the inflation rate, providing at least some profit potential in most parts of the country. If inflation soars again, homeowners should be well protected against its damage.

How Much Home Can You Afford?

The question of whether you can afford a home and, if so, how much home you can afford to buy has two parts. Any deal you might make depends on how much money you can afford as a down payment and how much you can safely shell out for monthly mortgage payments.

You can find the answer to the first part of the question—how much down payment can you muster—in the net-worth statement in Chapter 1. This inventory of your assets and liabilities will point the way to a realistic down payment and even show you where it might come from. Lenders usually want you to put down 10% to 20% of the purchase price of the property. Although it is possible to get a mortgage with a smaller down payment, if you buy with less than 20% down you'll probably be required to reduce the lender's risk by buying private

How Much Can You Spend for Housing?

I. Before you can know how big a mortgage payment you can afford, you need to tally your other monthly expenses. Do that on this worksheet. Then subtract the total on line B from the total on line A to see how much you have available for housing (line C).

Monthly Income		Recreation and vacation	$ _____
Take-home pay (after taxes)	$ _____	Telephone	$ _____
Other income	$ _____	Personal	$ _____
Total (A)	**$ _____**	Taxes	
		(not deducted from pay)	$ _____
Monthly Nonhousing Outlays		Savings	$ _____
Food and household		Charity	$ _____
supplies	$ _____	Other	$ _____
Transportation	$ _____	**Total (B)**	**$ _____**
Insurance	$ _____		
Health care	$ _____	**Amount Available for Housing**	
Clothing and cleaning	$ _____	Monthly income (A)	$ _____
Education	$ _____	Nonhousing expenses (B)	$ _____
Debt and installment		**Amount available (C)**	**$ _____**
payments	$ _____		

II. Now, with the figure on line C in mind, plus a firm idea of the size of the down payment you plan to make, you're ready to begin comparing individual homes using the simple worksheet below. Real estate agents or current owners can give you reasonably precise estimates for the expenses listed there. Under "other" you might include any additional cost of commuting to work from that location, or new expenses such as community association fees. If you would reduce any of your current nonhousing expenses by buying a particular home, estimate your savings and subtract that amount from anticipated expenses. Then add up the housing costs and compare line D with line C. If C is larger than D, you've probably found a place you can afford. Chapter 6 describes how the type of mortgage you choose can often be tailored to the resources you have available.

Anticipated Monthly Housing Expenses

Mortgage payment	$ _____	Maintenance and repairs	$ _____
Insurance	$ _____	(figure at least 1% of the price per year)	
Property taxes	$ _____	Other	$ _____
Utilities	$ _____	**Total (D)**	**$ _____**

mortgage insurance (PMI). First-year premiums range from about 0.5% of the loan amount to 1% or so, depending on the size of the loan and the size of your down payment, among other things. As the years go by and your loan balance is paid down, and rising home values boost your equity above 20%, you can ask the lender to drop the PMI.

One more point about down payments: If you plan to use a gift of money from family or friends, you'll find that lenders may expect at least a 5% cash down payment from your own resources in addition to any funds you receive as a gift.

What Kind of Home Should You Buy?

The best preparation for home buying is to inventory not just your financial resources but also your likes and dislikes. Start with the general—your price range and approximate location—and then move to the specific: neighborhood, age and type of home, and kind of ownership (traditional, condominium or cooperative).

Most important, focus on the location and quality of the property. Don't go chasing an exact price or a particular feature. Price is negotiable, and a good-quality home in a good location is probably a better buy in the long run than a "perfect" home that has the bad luck to be in a lousy location.

Walking into a real estate office with a list of features you consider necessary in a home and a neighborhood will help guide the agent and save you the time of looking at homes that don't fit your needs.

It wouldn't hurt to draw up a list of dislikes, as well. Think of all the houses and apartments that for one reason or another made a negative impression on you, and try to identify exactly what it was you didn't like. Also consider things that other buyers might not like. Heavy traffic on the street might not bother you, but it will make resale tougher. You might not mind the 28 steep steps up to the front door, but they surely will turn away some potential future buyers.

Starting From Scratch

Buying a home that hasn't been built yet, whether it's being custom-built for you or is part of a new development, takes some special care.

Before you sign any contract, thoroughly check out the builder. You are counting on the builder's reputation. Check it with the Better Business Bureau. Make sure the company is a member in good standing of the local builders association.

Next, find a recently completed development the same builder has worked on. Attend a homeowners meeting if you can, or talk to several owners about their dealings with the builder. Ask if they are satisfied with the way complaints have been handled and whether necessary repairs were made in a reasonable amount of time. Would they buy another home from the builder? The answer to that question should carry a lot of weight.

Here are some actions to take before deciding whether to buy a home that's still on the drawing boards.

Concerning the development:

- Contact the city or county planning department to see the master plan filed by your builder.

- Find out if other developments are planned for empty land surrounding the property you're considering.

- Talk to local school officials to learn about the adequacy of current facilities and plans for future construction.

Concerning the homeowners association:

- Get a copy of the association's rules.

- Review the financial statements to see if adequate reserves have been established to maintain existing facilities (like swimming pools, tennis courts or a community center) or to build new ones.

- Find out how high the association dues are and whether there are limits to the amount they can be raised each year.

Concerning your contract with the builder:

- Make sure that all upgrades and features are listed.

- Include a clause that allows you to visit the site on several occasions during the construction process (you'll probably have to be accompanied by a builder's representative).

- Remember that you don't have to accept the builder's contract as is; negotiating is expected, so do it. A typical deposit is 5%, but you may be able to get it lowered. If the market is slow, you should be able to get the builder to throw in some upgrades, but in fast-selling markets don't expect any concessions.

- Be sure to make the deal contingent on your ability to get mortgage financing, and ask the builder to provide at least 30 days' notice before closing. Try to get the builder to hold your deposit in escrow (this is common in some areas of the country, but you may have a fight on your hand in other areas).

Concerning the condition of the house:
- Inspect everything in the home—try the faucets, flush toilets, turn on the heat and the air-conditioning. If you're not comfortable doing it yourself, hire a home inspector. They normally inspect older homes, but there is no reason they can't inspect a new one.

Buying a Condo or Co-op

Condos and co-ops are legal forms of ownership, not any particular kind of building. In a condominium, the owners of individual dwelling units hold title to their own units and own a proportional interest in the land and common areas of the development. Garden apartments, high-rises and townhouses are the most common forms that condominiums take, but the category can also include detached houses, beach houses, offices and warehouses. The common property may belong to the condo developer at first, but eventually it is conveyed to an owners association. Thereafter the development is controlled and operated by directors of the condo owners association, often through a hired manager. Condominiums can be purchased with conventional and government-backed mortgages.

In a cooperative, residents do not hold title to their individual units. Instead they own shares of stock in a corporation that owns the development. They are, in effect, tenants of the corporation entitled to occupancy by virtue of their ownership of stock.

You normally can't get a mortgage to buy a co-op. Instead you get a "share loan," which is similar to a mortgage, except that it is somewhat more expensive and harder to find. In addition to loan payments to the lender, co-op residents make monthly maintenance payments to the cooperative corporation, which pays for the mortgage on the building, real estate taxes and general upkeep. As a partial owner of the corporation, you can deduct your proportional share of the corporation's mortgage interest and taxes on your income-tax return.

Advantages and Amenities—at a Price

Many condos and co-ops have amenities that few residents could afford on their own—swimming pools, saunas, game rooms, tennis courts, even golf courses. Usually, lawns are mowed, leaves raked and shrubbery trimmed by hired hands. Condos and co-ops often cost less than detached houses in comparable locations. You have a say in how the development is run.

All this comes at a price. You're required to pay your share of the cost of all the luxuries, and you can't put off paying monthly fees or special assessments the way you can postpone maintenance or repairs on an individual home. You probably have less space than in a detached house. You can't enlarge your unit. You are subject to strict rules adopted by the majority of owners. Certain activities and hobbies, such as gun collecting or amateur radio (with its three-story antennas), may be banned or restricted. Some developments ban pets.

Condos tend not to appreciate as rapidly as single-family homes. If you live in an area of rapid development, you should be aware that if you need to sell your condo, you'll be competing with new units that are springing up around you.

You're also dependent on directors and professional managers to maintain both reserve funds and the property itself. If they fail to do their jobs, then the building or grounds could deteriorate and you could lose some, or all, of your equity.

Shopping Tips for Condos and Co-ops

Buy the largest unit that you can afford. A townhouse will have more of a market than a two-bedroom apartment, and a two-bedroom apartment will fare better on resale than a one-bedroom.

Look for a unit that has a special location—proximity to the pool might appeal to young families or a serene park view to an older couple. If something sets your unit apart from others, it'll work to your benefit when you want to sell and there are ten other units in your development on the market.

If you're considering an apartment-style condo or co-op, pay close attention to potential problems with reserves and assessments—even though that means wading through detailed records. Insufficient reserves can have wrenching financial consequences if there's an emergency. Find out whether the association has accumulated adequate reserves to pay for major repairs and to replace worn-out equipment. As buildings age, residents must be prepared for such expenses as replacing the roof, upgrading the electrical system and installing a new boiler.

Monthly assessments can be expected to rise as time goes by, so look for a record of reasonable increases. Assessments should be large enough to cover routine maintenance and still permit the buildup of reserves. Some condos and co-ops choose to deal with big repair bills by imposing special assessments rather than accumulating the necessary cash in a reserve fund. If you buy into a building in which residents have postponed needed work, remember: The repairs lie ahead—at your expense.

Generally, the best locations are residential areas that have a good mix of quality apartment buildings and homes in the middle to upper price range, with rising property values. Make sure that the area provides easy access to public transportation, stores, hospitals and parks, and that it boasts a highly rated public school system. Check out zoning regulations for the land surrounding the development, and try to visualize the neighborhood in five, ten and 15 years. You don't want the wooded view from your living-room window turned into a six-lane highway in five years.

Take note of the vacancy rate and the supply-demand situation in the area. A glut of empty units or a high percentage of renters can affect property values in a general area or in a particular building.

Are rentals necessarily bad? Not if you live in a resort community. But potential buyers in developments with less than an 80% owner-occupancy rate will have difficulty getting mortgages, which cuts down the potential market.

Especially for Condos

Find out who owns the common facilities—the swimming pool, tennis courts, parking areas and laundry room, for example. If the developer owns these (and leases them to the development), it means that your fees could escalate at his discretion, rather than the condo board's. And check out the facilities themselves to make sure they are adequate for the number of residents.

Walk around and decide if you'll fit in with the other residents. Are you considerably older or younger than most? Perhaps you have young children and most of the residents are single professionals, leaving your kids without playmates.

If you're comfortable with what you've found so far, look into the condo's rules and regulations, which you'll find in the master deed, bylaws or house rules—all documents that the builder or owner must give you. Study them carefully; once you sign the purchase contract, you've explicitly and contractually agreed to abide by the regulations that will be imposed upon you and other residents by the condo or co-op association. Strangely enough, too few rules can lead to problems down the road, but you have to be sure you can live with the ones that exist.

Finally, investigate the financial condition of the condo association, which you can learn from examining the documents that must be given to potential buyers. What debts does it have and to whom are they owed? Are the reserve funds adequate to handle both routine maintenance and replacement of such expensive items as roofs and furnaces? Is the association quick to impose special assessments to cover emergency needs?

Especially for Co-ops

Co-op buyers need to ask many of the same questions as prospective condo buyers. In addition, you'll want to find out about the age and condition of the building; ask to see an engineering report on the condition of the property (if one is available). If the building is more than 40 years old, for example, the plumbing system may need to be replaced. How would the co-op board cover the expense? Are there sufficient reserves to pay for it or will owners receive a special assessment?

Cooperative corporations whose shares can be bought using share loans (see page 62) must meet minimum standards for structural soundness, restricted commercial use and appropriate management. In addition, approved projects must have adequate cash flows and monthly assessments sufficient to meet current operating costs and to build reserve funds.

As a prospective co-op buyer, you may be asked to meet with members of the co-op's board of governors. You could be asked to submit financial records and personal references. But no matter how selective the co-op residents are, federal law and many state statutes prohibit them from rejecting or discouraging prospective buyers on the basis of race, gender, creed or national origin.

The National Association of Housing Cooperatives, 1401 New York Avenue N.W., Suite 1100, Washington, D.C. 20005-2160 (202-737-0797 or www.coophousing.org) can provide general information on buying into a cooperative.

The National Cooperative Bank, which makes loans to co-op tenant-shareholders, has a helpful brochure available. *Co-op Housing Buying and Financing - A Consumer's Guide*. Call the NCB at 800–322–1251, or write to 139 S. High St., Hillsboro, OH 45133. You may also view the publication online at www.ncb.com.

How to Get Your Money's Worth From a Real Estate Agent

You need to know the ropes when dealing with a real estate agent. Both buyer and seller face a major financial decision. A buyer wants the most house for the money; a seller wants the most money for the house. A good real estate agent can guide events toward a mutually beneficial conclusion. A bad one can make an already stressful situation worse.

What can you reasonably expect an agent to do for you? Do you really need one? How much should you pay? What recourse do you have if something goes wrong?

It's helpful to learn the lingo first. *Agent* is the commonly used term for a salesperson who is licensed to work for a real estate broker. A *broker* is licensed to conduct a real estate business and to negotiate transactions for a fee. Both may properly be called agents because they act as agents for clients. Some brokers and agents may be called Realtors. Realtors (note the capital "R"—it's a trade name) and Realtor Associates (who work for a Realtor) are members of the National Association of Realtors, a trade and lobbying organization.

Whom the Agent Works for

Unwary home buyers may innocently divulge their strategies to the wrong real estate agent. If you are working with anyone other than a buyer's broker, such disclosure is a big mistake because the agent works for the seller and may be obliged to report on your conversation.

A seller's agent can help you with information about market conditions, neighborhoods, schools, public facilities, tax rates, zoning laws, proposed roads and construction, and other essentials for evaluating your purchase. No agent can know everything about a property, but an honest one will tell you about problems he or she is aware of. And an agent could be held accountable for providing wrong information on something he or she ought to know about. (A buyer could also sue an owner who conceals known defects.)

Does a buyer really need an agent? Almost certainly. As a househunter on your own, you're at a disadvantage. Unless you are thoroughly familiar with a given area, you'll miss an agent's knowledge and resources. You also won't have access to the computer multiple listing service (MLS) of houses for sale, through which participating brokers share information on listings.

Buyer's Brokers

The conflict of interest created by an agent's need to represent both the buyer and seller but being paid by the seller has led to the creation of buyer's brokers. When you hire a buyer's broker, you enter into a "single agency" relationship—the broker is hired by you and represents only you, having no allegiance to the seller.

Buyer's brokers can be paid by the hour, by a flat fee negotiated up front, or by a percentage of the purchase price. Try to avoid the latter, because there's obviously less incentive to negotiate a lower price on your behalf. Don't enter this relationship thinking you'll save money. With low- to mid-priced homes, you will pay the equivalent of a 3% commission. On higher-end homes, there will probably be some saving over the standard commission rate.

There are some obvious advantages to dealing with a buyer's broker. You needn't fear discussing your buying strategy with your agent or asking for advice on your opening offer. Because the agent represents you alone, not the seller, and preferably works for a flat fee, any conflict of interest is eliminated. The buyer's broker is free to negotiate the best possible price and terms for you.

To find a buyer's broker in your area, ask your local Board of Realtors or large real estate firms for referrals, or contact one of the following:

- **The Buyer's Agent Inc.** (1255 Lynnfield Road, Suite 273, Memphis, TN 38119; www.forbuyers.com; 800–766–8728), is a franchise operating in 28 states. It represents buyers on a fee or commission basis.

- **The National Association of Exclusive Buyer Agents** (NAEBA; 320 West Sabal Palm Place, Suite 1505, Longwood, FL 32779; www.naeba.com; 800-500-3569) is a consumer-advocacy and professional training organization that can provide information on the role of an exclusive buyer's agent as well as names of agents in your area.

Dual Agency

A real estate agent who serves both the buyer and the seller, acting only as an intermediary, is known as a dual agent. The dual agent can't advise you on negotiating tactics, nor can he pass along confidential information to the other party. Compensation for a dual agent is based on commission—so once again there is incentive to get the highest possible price.

Some real estate firms appoint different agents to represent the buyer and seller; some represent only the seller on properties they list and only the buyer on properties listed by other firms; and some allow agents to represent both.

What's best for you? If you're familiar with the real estate market and are comfortable negotiating on your own behalf, then a dual agent will be fine. On the other hand, if you want some help from an agent or advice on tactics, your best bet is hiring a buyer's broker to represent you.

What It Takes to Get a Mortgage

So you've figured out how much house you can afford, and the kind of home you'd like to buy. Now it's time to give serious thought to finding a mortgage.

The mantra for mortgage shopping is simple: Focus on the loan, not the lender. Concern yourself with interest rates, points, processing costs and other variables that affect the cost of the loan. Don't worry much about where the lender is located—your mortgage will be sold once or twice before you're done, anyway. Study the pros and cons of fixed-rate and adjustable-rate borrowing. Learn the lingo so you can ask the questions that lead you to the best deal.

Before you can worry about comparing mortgages, you need to worry about qualifying in the first place. How will lenders evaluate your application?

The answer is pretty much the same wherever you live. Lenders want to play by the rules set by Fannie Mae or Freddie Mac. These government-sponsored organizations buy up mortgages from lenders, repackage them as securities and then resell them to investors.

By selling their mortgages to Fannie Mae or Freddie Mac, lenders convert their loans to cash, with which they can make more loans. Fannie and Freddie insist that the mortgages they buy meet certain standards, which lenders are anxious to meet. If they don't, they risk being unable to sell their loans and thus replenish their supply of lendable cash.

Fannie Mae measures your borrowing power by matching your projected housing expenses to your household income. Principal and interest payments, property taxes and homeowners insurance—what lenders refer to as PITI—should total no more than 28% of your gross monthly income. *And* that monthly house payment plus other debts with ten or more monthly payments still outstanding (that could include automobile or student loans) should total no more than 36% of your gross income.

Gross income is what you and your spouse earn before taxes for work that you have been doing for a year or longer. Income from the extra job you took a few weeks before applying for the loan doesn't count. Other income—such as bonuses, commissions and overtime pay—must be averaged over two years to be considered wages. You can count alimony and child-support payments as income if the payments will continue for at least three years from the date of your loan application.

Not all loans get the straight 28/36 treatment. To qualify for certain adjustable-rate mortgages (ARMs), you'll be expected to meet stricter requirements for the first year's payments because they are typically lower than second and subsequent years' payments. Loans with low down payments also draw tougher scrutiny. On the other hand, a down payment of 20% or more may earn you a 33/38 ratio instead of 28/36. FHA and VA mortgages also get higher ratios because they are backed by the federal government.

Debt ratios are only guidelines, and 30% to 40% of the loans Fannie Mae buys exceed the guidelines because other factors can tip the scales. It counts in your favor if you have a good credit history, make a substantial down payment, possess liquid assets equal to at least three months of home payments, or have in the past paid a large proportion of your income for rent or toward a mortgage.

The worksheet on page 59 will help you assess your home-buying potential. If you anticipate sizable financial obligations, your employment outlook is uncertain, your down-payment fund is low, your family is likely to grow, or you'll need money for improvements or furnishings, prudence suggests spending less per month than the calculations indicate you can afford.

With some idea of how you'll be judged by lenders, you're ready to go shopping for a mortgage. But first you've got to know the language of these loans.

Loan Lingo: Interest and Points

Lenders charge for mortgages two ways: with interest and with "points." You pay interest for the life of the loan, but you pay the points up front. They may be called a loan discount fee or a loan origination fee. Other mortgage-related charges nickel-and-dime you in several ways, as we'll see later, but interest and points constitute your biggest mortgage burdens.

One point equals 1% of the loan amount. Because a point is prepaid interest, it raises the effective interest rate of the loan. Look at it this way: If you borrow $100,000 and pay two points, or $2,000, to get the loan, the lender has actually laid out only $98,000. But you'll have to pay back the full $100,000 face value of the loan, plus interest. In effect, you've given the lender a discount off the face amount of the

---

Important Tax Angles of Homeownership

Uncle Sam is a silent but generous partner in homeownership. First he subsidizes your mortgage payments, then he deliberately overlooks part or all of the profits you make when you sell. But this generosity has a price, and a misstep on your part can have expensive consequences. Following are some answers to the kinds of questions that come up when people buy and sell homes—and while they own them.

Deducting Mortgage Interest

Q: Is there a limit on the amount of interest a homeowner can deduct?

A: All the interest on debt you take on to build or buy a principal residence and second residence is deductible on loans totaling up to $1 million. The $1-million ceiling on this so-called acquisition debt includes money you borrow to renovate your home.

Q: What are the rules for deducting interest on home-equity loans?

A: Interest on home-equity loans is deductible up to $100,000, no matter how you use the money.

Q: We have completely paid off the mortgage on our home, which is now worth $200,000. We want to take out a new mortgage to renovate the kitchen and add a small wing to the house for guests. The estimated cost will be $110,000. In addition, we intend to borrow $10,000 for a car. Since I'll be borrowing more than $100,000, will the extra $20,000 debt be nondeductible?

A. Interest on the entire loan is deductible. Because you have no other mortgage on the property, the $110,000 borrowed for renovations is considered acquisition debt, subject to the $1-million ceiling. The $10,000 for the car qualifies as home-equity debt and counts against the $100,000 limit.

Q: We refinanced our mortgage and were told that we wouldn't be able to deduct all the points we paid. Somehow we're supposed to write it off a little at a time. Will the proper amount be included in the interest the bank reports we paid each year, or is there a special way to figure it out?

mortgage. Thus points are sometimes referred to as a discount fee. Just remember that the discount goes to the lender, not to you.

One point is roughly equivalent to an additional one-eighth of one percentage point (0.125%) on the interest rate of a 30-year fixed-rate mortgage. Thus an 8%, 30-year fixed-rate mortgage with no points is about equivalent to a 7% loan with eight points. Of course, lenders never charge that many points on a loan. After all, how many borrowers could afford to pay so much additional cash on top of their

A: It's an extra deduction and you have to figure it out yourself. The IRS considers points paid to refinance a mortgage to be prepaid interest and says they must be deducted proportionately over the life of the loan. If you paid $3,000 in points on a 15-year mortgage, for example, $200 would be deductible each year. If you refinanced around midyear and made six payments, your first-year deduction would be $100. Don't include the amount as part of the mortgage-interest deduction. Claim it on the indicated line of Schedule A.

Q: We recently inherited some money, enough to pay off the mortgage on our home. If we do so, we'll be stuck with a prepayment penalty. Would it be deductible?
A: Yes. Prepayment penalties are treated as interest and may be deducted in the year paid.

Deduct Commissions?
Q: We sold our home for $125,000, and the real estate commission took $7,500 of it. Can we deduct this charge on our taxes?
A: Sorry, but no.

Tax-Free Profits
Q: Is the law that allows tax-free profit when you sell homes as good as it sounds? Any traps in it?
A: Yes, it is as good as it sounds, and yes, there may be a trap or two in it. The law now allows single sellers filing an individual return to earn up to $250,000 in profit on a principal residence and not owe a penny of tax. For couples filing a joint return, the figure is a generous $500,000. There is no age requirement to meet, and you can invoke this break again and again, as long as you don't use it more than once in a two-year period. This applies to all sales after May 6, 1997. To qualify, you must have lived in the home for at least two of the five years leading up to the sale. One catch to be aware of if you have an office at home: Any portion of your house that qualifies for home-office tax deductions doesn't qualify for the tax-free profit. In such a case, you might want to stop claiming home office deductions for at least two of the five years leading up to the sale. That would allow the entire home to qualify as your principal residence.

Chapter Five • **71**

down payment? Not many. So instead of insisting on so much cash up front, lenders bump up the stated interest rate on the loan. That 7% mortgage with eight points becomes, in the marketplace, a 7.5% mortgage with four points, or a 7.625% mortgage with three points, or a 7.875% mortgage with one point. In the end, these are all the same; the only difference is when you pay the money.

How Points Raise the Rate

Stated Rate	Points	Effective Rate Over 5 years	Over 30 years
8%	3	8.6%	8.38%
8.25	2	8.65	8.50
8.375	1.5	8.675	8.56

Which is better, a lower-rate loan with several points or a higher-rate loan with no points? The answer depends on how long you'll be paying on the loan. Over time, the money you save with a lower rate (and thus lower monthly payments) will amount to more than you shelled out in points to get the lower rate. In general, the longer you'll be in the home, the better off you'll be paying more points up front to get the lower rate for the long term. A three-step calculation can help you choose the best combination of rates and points:
• First, estimate the number of years you'll be paying on the loan.
• Second, divide the years into the number of points.
• Third, add that to the interest rate and compare with other offers.

Say, for example, that you expect to be paying on the mortgage for five years. One lender offers an 8% loan with three points, another offers an 8.25% loan with two points, and a third offers an 8.375% loan with 1.5 points. Which is the best deal?

Over one year, those three points boost the effective rate of the 8% loan up to 11% (three points added to 8%). The 8.25% loan with two points works out to 10.25%, and the 8.375% loan with 1.5 points translates to 9.875%. But over five years, as you'll see in the table above, the loan with the lowest interest rate is the best deal even with those additional points. And the longer the loan runs, the bigger the advantage of the loan with the lowest rate. The table also shows the effective rate over 30 years.

Points go with the territory in the mortgage business, so you'll have to live with them (although sometimes you can shave them through negotiation). To compare different loans at different interest rates with different numbers of points tacked on to them, get from each lender the annual percentage rate (APR) of the loans you're considering. The APR takes points and other incidentals into account. But in weighing whether to pay more points to get a lower-rate loan, don't forget to consider how long you'll be paying on the loan.

Loan Lingo:
The Different Kinds of Mortgages

Mortgages come in lots of flavors. The standard fixed-rate variety—with its preset, life-of-the-mortgage, monthly payments covering principal repayment and interest—offers the peace of mind that comes with a predictable monthly check-writing exercise. But if interest rates fall, the holder of a fixed-rate mortgage is stuck with the higher rate unless he or she refinances.

On the other hand, if rates rise, it's the lender who's stuck. Who wants to be holding a vault full of 7% mortgages when rates are at 10%? In fact, the reluctance of lenders to make fixed-rate mortgage loans in a climate of rising interest rates in the late '70s led to the creation of the adjustable-rate mortgage (ARM). With an ARM, the interest rate you pay rises and falls with other interest rates throughout the economy, thus passing the risk of rising rates from the lender to the borrower. In exchange, you get a lower rate to begin with.

Which kind of mortgage do you want? Let's take a closer look at these two major types and their various incarnations.

30-Year Fixed-Rate Loans
This is the most familiar mortgage. The interest rate—and your monthly payments—remains the same for the life of the loan.

Shorter-Term Fixed-Rate Loans
Fifteen- and 20-year fixed-rate loans have become popular for home buyers who can afford the higher monthly payments. The loan is paid off faster than with a 30-year loan, and interest rates are usually one-half to one percentage point lower. A 15-year loan lets you own your home free and clear in half the time and for less than half the total

How Much Will the Payments Be?

This table will help you figure the monthly payment required per $1,000 of mortgage amount at various interest rates for three common mortgage terms. The numbers shown include principal and interest only; insurance and property taxes would be additional. To determine the monthly payment for a mortgage you're considering, multiply the appropriate amount in the table by the number of thousands of dollars involved. Example: $80,000 at 8% for 30 years would be 80 x 7.34, or $587.20 per month for principal and interest.

Interest Rate	15 Years	20 Years	30 Years
4.00%	7.40	6.06	4.77
4.25	7.52	6.19	4.92
4.50	7.65	6.33	5.07
4.75	7.78	6.46	5.22
5.00	7.91	6.60	5.37
5.25	8.04	6.74	5.52
5.50	8.17	6.88	5.68
5.75	8.30	7.02	5.84
6.00	8.44	7.17	6.00
6.25	8.58	7.31	6.16
6.50	8.72	7.46	6.33
6.75	8.85	7.61	6.49
7.00	8.99	7.76	6.66
7.25	9.13	7.91	6.83
7.50	9.28	8.06	7.00
7.75	9.42	8.21	7.17
8.00	9.56	8.37	7.34
8.25	9.71	8.53	7.52
8.50	9.85	8.68	7.69
8.75	10.00	8.84	7.87
9.00	10.15	9.00	8.05
9.25	10.30	9.16	8.23
9.50	10.45	9.33	8.41
9.75	10.60	9.49	8.60
10.00	10.75	9.66	8.78
10.25	10.90	9.82	8.97
10.50	11.06	9.99	9.15
10.75	11.21	10.16	9.34
11.00	11.37	10.33	9.53
11.25	11.53	10.50	9.72
11.50	11.69	10.67	9.91
11.75	11.85	10.84	10.10
12.00	12.01	11.02	10.29

interest cost of a 30-year fixed-rate loan. But when it comes to calculating the monthly payments, the slightly lower interest rate isn't enough to cancel the effect of the shorter repayment period. The higher monthly payments can be burdensome, especially for first-time buyers. On a 15-year, $100,000 mortgage at 7%, the monthly payments are $899—about $200 more than for a 30-year, 7.5% mortgage for the same amount.

Adjustable-Rate Mortgages

The interest rate on an ARM changes periodically in sync with an index selected by the lender. The adjustment interval may be every six months, or once a year, or once every three, five or seven years. At adjustment time (or, more accurately, on the calculation date, which will be a month or so before the actual adjustment date), the lender looks at the index rate and slaps on a margin—typically two to three percentage points—to come up with the new rate.

Interest rates being paid on one-, three- and five-year Treasury securities are commonly used as ARM indexes. The Federal Housing Finance Board's National Average Contract Mortgage Rate, often called the FHB Series of Closed Loans, is also popular with lenders. The Federal COFI (Cost of Funds Index) and the Eleventh District COFI are used by lenders throughout the country even though the latter is based on interest rates in California, Arizona and Nevada.

Some indexes are more volatile than others, and the COFIs are generally the least volatile. They are listed in the business pages of major newspapers, or you can follow them—and other common rates—by calling the Yield and Commitment Information Hotline sponsored by Fannie Mae (800–752–7020 or www.fanniemae.com).

Find out which index will be used in any ARM you are considering. It is impossible to predict which index will move most in your favor. When rates decline, you want to benefit as quickly as possible. One-year Treasury securities will do that for you. When rates rise, you'd be better off with a slower-moving index, such as five-year Treasuries.

Most ARMs have limits, or caps, on rate changes. When interest rates are rising rapidly, caps protect you from huge jumps in your monthly payments. Most ARMs have both periodic ceilings (limiting the increase from one adjustment period to the next) and lifetime ceilings (limiting the overall interest-rate increase over the term of the loan). Limits of two percentage points on annual increases, with a lifetime cap of six points, are typical. Caps work the other way, too. If

Checklist for Comparing ARMs

After you've prequalified for the amount of money you can borrow, use this worksheet to assess different lenders' adjustable-rate mortgage (ARM) offerings. Make yourself a copy for each lender.

Lender's name _____
Telephone number _____
Down payment required _____ %
Beginning interest rate (APR) _____ %
Points _____ %
Beginning payment $ _____
Lifetime cap on interest rate _____ %
Periodic cap on the interest rate? ❏ yes ❏ no
What is the cap? _____ %
How often can payment be adjusted? _____
Is there a cap on payment? ❏ yes ❏ no
What is the cap? _____ %
Does loan permit negative amortization? ❏ yes ❏ no
   How much negative amortization is allowed
   relative to the original loan amount? _____
   (For example, can mortgage balance grow to
   105% of original loan, 110%, and so on?)
Loan is tied to which index?
   ❏ 1-year Treasury securities ❏ 3-year Treasury securities
   ❏ 5-year Treasury securities ❏ Other: _____
   ❏ Federal Housing Board's National Average Contract Rate
     series for closed loans
Number of adjustments loan calls for _____
   First adjustment occurs _____ months/years
   Second adjustment occurs _____ months/years
   Third adjustment occurs _____ months/years
Can loan be converted to a fixed-rate? ❏ yes ❏ no
   Under what circumstances? _____
   Cost of conversion option? $ _____
Can loan be prepaid in whole or in part at anytime without penalty?
   ❏ yes ❏ no
   If yes, what are the conditions? _____
   Is loan assumable by a qualified buyer? ❏ yes ❏ no

How ARM Payments Could Go Up Or Down

Say you have a $100,000 one-year adjustable-rate mortgage (ARM) with an initial rate of 4%, an annual cap of two percentage points, and a lifetime cap of five percentage points. Here's what the monthly payment would be on a fully amortized loan if payments were adjusted up every year to the maximum and then remained at that level for the life of the loan.

Year	Rate	Years of Amortization	Monthly Payment	Principal Balance at End of Period
1	4%	30	$477.42	$98,238.85
2	6	29	596.32	96,942.11
3	8	28	723.92	95,975.45
4	9	27	790.00	95,097.70
5-30	9	26	790.00	—

And this is what the monthly payments would be if interest rates on a $100,000, 7½% ARM dropped one-half percentage point every year for five years:

Year	Rate	Years of Amortization	Monthly Payment	Principal Balance at End of Period
1	7.5%	30	$699.21	$99,078.15
2	7.0	29	665.93	97,987.84
3	6.5	28	634.00	96,711.39
4	6.0	27	603.46	95,232.24
5	5.5	26	574.39	93,534.91
6-30	5.0	25	546.80	—

rates plunge between adjustments, the limits protect the lender from drastic drops in the payments you have to make.

ARMs with *payment* caps rather than *rate* caps limit your monthly payment increase at the time of each adjustment, typically to a certain percentage of the previous payment. They can create negative amortization when rising interest rates would dictate payments higher than the cap permits. The difference in such cases is added to the loan principal, and as a result your indebtedness can actually grow while you think you're paying off the loan. ARMs with payment caps are rarely offered today and should be avoided.

Convertible ARMs

Some ARMs can be converted to fixed-rate loans. You might want the right to convert in the future—say, after two or three years—if you expect rates will be lower then. If the cost is the same, you should always pick a convertible ARM over a nonconvertible one. But costs usually aren't the same. You'll have to pay a conversion fee and probably a slightly higher rate to start, for example. That makes a convertible ARM a good idea only if you are convinced that rates will be lower in the future (as might be the case if you are getting the mortgage during an unusual period of high inflation, for example) and you plan to stay in the same place long enough to benefit from a conversion.

FHA Loans

The Federal Housing Administration insures a wide variety of mortgages. FHA insurance was conceived as a way to assist low-income home buyers by encouraging lenders to make loans to them, and the debt-to-income ratios are more generous than they are for other loans. Still, even high-income buyers can get FHA loans. The maximum loan amount varies somewhat from one geographic area to another, depending on local housing prices. The FHA insures fixed-rate loans and ARMs.

Because FHA loans are insured by a federal agency, they are practically risk-free to lenders and should carry an interest rate a bit below the going market rate. Down payments can be 5% or less for buyers who will live in their homes themselves. The buyer must pay the cost of FHA insurance, which has recently been 2.25%. It is collected at the time of settlement, but you can increase the size of your mortgage to cover the cost and roll it into your monthly payment.

Veterans' Loans

The Department of Veterans Affairs guarantees lenders against losses on mortgages taken out by eligible veterans. The primary advantage of such a mortgage is that no down payment is required unless a veteran is obtaining a loan with a graduated-payment feature or the loan amount requested is more than the agency thinks the property is worth. The VA guarantees conventional 30-year mortgages, as well as graduated-payment mortgages, growing-equity mortgages and other types of loans.

In the past, mortgage rates were set by the VA. Rates are now set by lenders, not by the government. The VA permits veterans to pay points but not to finance them in their loans. The VA collects from the buyer a one-time funding fee of 2% of the loan amount at settlement. This pays for the guarantee and will be reduced a bit if you make a down payment.

It's important to understand that the VA is not guaranteeing the entire mortgage. It will guarantee no more than about $50,000. In general, lenders insist that the guarantee, plus your down payment, cover at least 25% of the loan amount. Thus, as a practical matter, VA loans max out at about $200,000. Every dollar of down payment you can come up with boosts that ceiling by four dollars.

You can find out whether you qualify for a VA loan by calling or writing the nearest VA office. For general information, call 800–827–1000 for recorded messages describing the program. For specific information about eligibility, you will have to supply your military service number, social security number, birth date, date of entry into the service, date and place of separation, name of the unit you were with when discharged, and type of discharge.

Serious Mortgage Shopping

Begin your search for a mortgage with your real estate agent, who can provide you with a list of potential lenders from the broker's computerized loan origination (CLO) system. These lists don't necessarily cover everything, though, so you need to do some checking on your own. Begin by finding out the rates at your own bank, and then pick up the Yellow Pages and start calling independent mortgage companies, savings institutions, commercial banks and any credit unions to which you belong.

Simply ask for the current rate on the kind of loan you want—30-year fixed, ARM and so forth. Ask for the interest rate and the points, and how the size of the down payment might affect the rate. (Mortgage brokers can be helpful because they represent several different lenders. You pay for their service, so make sure you ask for the effective rate to you, net of the broker's fees.)

You can tell from the table on page 74 what your monthly payment would be for different interest rates. (Be aware, however, that the table calculates the payment for interest and principal only. Property taxes and insurance are extra and will vary according to the price of the house you're considering and where it is located.) And the worksheet on page 59 helped you determine how much you can afford. In about half an hour on the phone, you can do a pretty good job of surveying the lenders in your area. In some cities, the real estate sections of the newspaper do a lot of the work for you by publishing a list of lenders and their rates, usually once a week. The listing should tell you the name and phone number of the mortgage reporting service that compiled the data. Call that number for a more complete list. There may be a small charge.

But don't stop there. Mortgage lending is a national business these days, so you can conduct a national search for the best rate. The fastest way to do it is online. If you don't have access to the Internet, ask your broker to help or make a trip to a computer-equipped friend's house or a large public library. The following sites can be especially helpful. Each carries up-to-date listings of lenders and rates, as well as general mortgage information, calculators and other helpful tools for mortgage shoppers.

HSH Associates (www.hsh.com). Provides mortgage rates, averages by city and state, calculators and links to lenders.

HomePath (www.homepath.com). Sponsored by Fannie Mae, this site lists mortgage lenders in all areas, and provides general information on home and mortgage shopping.

iOwn® (www.iown.com). Lists rates from the nation's largest mortgage lenders and brokers, allows online mortgage applications and provides listings of comparable recent sales in neighborhoods where you might be shopping for a home.

Kiplinger.com (www.kiplinger.com). Click on "Tools" for help in comparing mortgages. Click on "Find a Mortgage" for a link to the *BankRate Monitor* Web site (www.bankrate.com), which follows competitive rates in all 50 states and Washington, D.C., with credit news and helpful calculators.

RateNet (www.rate.net). Keeps tabs on 9,000 lenders in 175 markets and finds the ten best rates in your area.

When you've selected a lender, find out how long the advertised or quoted rate remains effective. Some lenders guarantee the rate for 45 days or 60 days, but others offer no guarantee. If rates have been rising and experts predict that they will hold or continue to rise for the foreseeable future, consider locking in the rate with a loan commitment. The lock-in guarantees you the rate quoted at the time of application for a specific period of time, in exchange for a fee. The longer the lock-in period, the higher the fee you'll have to pay.

Get a Home Inspection

When drawing up an offer on your dream home, be sure you make the contract contingent on a professional home inspection satisfactory to you. Such a clause provides you with an "out" in case the inspection uncovers a serious problem with the house that you didn't see.

A thorough home inspection covers the structural integrity of the house, the roof, siding and other exterior features, interior walls and doors, kitchens and bathrooms, the electrical system, heating and air-conditioning systems, and the plumbing. If the home has a swimming pool, tennis court, well or septic system, you'll need to arrange for a separate inspection.

How to Find a Good Home Inspector

Begin by asking friends and associates for referrals. Consider inspectors recommended by your real estate agent, but make sure the inspectors don't work for the agent or for a contractor looking to drum up repair jobs. Ask to see a couple of completed inspection reports. Look for an inspector who writes up thorough reports on current problems as well as problems you may encounter in the future. You don't want an inspector whose idea of a report is just preprinted forms with checked-off boxes.

Try to find an inspector who is a member of the American Society of Home Inspectors (ASHI). This group sets the standards for the industry—requiring its members to pass a series of exams, perform 250 fee-paid inspections meeting ASHI standards and complete 60 hours of continuing education every three years (ASHI, 932 Lee St., Suite 101, Des Plaines, IL 60016; 800–743–2744; www.ashi.com). The National Institute of Building Inspectors, founded by the HouseMaster of America Home Inspection Service (a franchise business), trains its inspectors according to the standards set by ASHI and requires its inspectors to carry liability insurance and meet certain continuing-education requirements (NIBI, 424 Vosseller Ave., Bound Brook, NJ 08805; 888–281–6424; www.nibi.com). Contact either organization for a list of inspectors in your area.

Go along for the inspection

Accompany the inspector as he tours the home. Expect this to take about two to three hours—and take advantage of the excellent opportunity to ask questions about both existing and potential problems, and to get estimates on repair costs. If the inspector finds serious problems, you can get out of the contract. If the inspector uncovers less serious problems, try to get the owner to pay for the repairs or adjust your original offer to reflect the cost of repairs.

Should You Refinance Your Mortgage?

A popular rule of thumb says you should consider refinancing your mortgage—that is, swapping the old one for a new one at a lower

---

Refinancing: How Much Would It Save?

This worksheet lets you figure out how long it would take to break even after the expenses of refinancing, and what your savings would be thereafter. The example is based on a fixed-rate $100,000 mortgage at 10% for 30 years, refinanced at 8% for 30 years.

	Our Example	Your Loan
The Cost of Refinancing		
1. Points	$1,000	$ _____
2. Application fee	35	_____
3. Title search and insurance	500	_____
4. Inspections	200	_____
5. Survey	150	_____
6. Lender's underwriting fee	200	_____
7. Credit report	50	_____
8. Appraisal	250	_____
9. Attorney fees	250	_____
10. Recording fees	50	_____
11. Transfer taxes	1,000	_____
12. Other fees	0	_____
Total Cost of Refinancing	**$3,685**	$ _____
The Payback		
1. Current monthly payment (P&I)	$878	$ _____
2. Subtract new monthly payment (P&I) (30-year fixed-rate at 8%)	–734	– _____
3. Pretax savings per month	144	_____
4. Multiply tax rate (e.g., 28%) by savings and subtract result	–40	– _____
5. After-tax savings per month	$104	$ _____
Number of Months to Break Even	35	_____
Divide monthly savings ($104) into total cost of refinancing ($3,685)		

---

82 Kiplinger • Major Money Decisions

rate—if you can cut the old rate by two percentage points or more. That's generally a solid guideline, but like all rules of thumb, it's not entirely reliable. If you're carrying a jumbo mortgage, for instance, or if you plan to stay put for many years, refinancing could be worthwhile with a smaller differential—say, one percentage point. The situation gets even more complicated when you compare fixed rates with ARMs or want to switch to a shorter-term loan.

Refinancing isn't free: You'll have to pay a lump sum up front, perhaps several thousand dollars, in exchange for those lower monthly payments. The key in any case is how long it will take you to pay yourself back. The worksheet on the opposite page shows you how to figure that out.

What If You Have an ARM?

If you have an adjustable-rate mortgage and plan to stay in your house for years to come, it could make sense to lock in a fixed rate. You won't necessarily save a lot of money compared with the ARM you're trading in, but you get the peace of mind of knowing you won't lose if rates rise. If you plan to sell within two or three years, stick with the ARM you've got. It could take several years to pay off the cost of refinancing via lower monthly payments, and in the meantime your annual adjustments will keep you within shouting distance of current rates, anyway.

Should you swap an old ARM for a new one?

First-year "teaser" rates make it tempting, but remember, after the first year, your interest rate would hover at about the level it would have been on your old ARM, assuming the index and the margin are the same. You come out ahead only if your first-year savings exceed the cost of refinancing. That's possible but unlikely.

Tax Facts for Refinancers

When you're refinancing just the balance of your mortgage, interest on the entire amount you borrow is tax-deductible. If you borrow additional money, the interest on up to $100,000 extra is also deductible, as home-equity debt.

Unlike points for the original mortgage, points for refinancing must be deducted on a pro-rata basis over the life of the loan, whether you pay them in cash or add them to the loan. For a 30-year loan, for instance, you deduct one-thirtieth of the total paid each year. Exception: If you use the funds for home improvements, the interest is considered to be paid on home-equity debt, and points are deductible in the year paid.

You can keep money in your pocket by folding the closing costs into the loan. This also has the effect of adding normally nondeductible charges, such as for an appraisal, to the amount on which you pay tax-deductible interest.

Chapter 6

Insuring Your Home

Homeowners insurance is one of those financial facts of life that just kind of happens to you. When you buy a home, the mortgage lender will insist on insurance coverage, so you get an agent's name, call up and buy a policy. Odds are the premiums are even paid from the same lender-controlled escrow account that pays your property tax. Out of sight, out of mind. You don't give homeowners insurance much thought—unless you try to file a claim and get into a squabble with the company.

The danger here is that insuring your home year after year becomes so routine that you fall prey to three potentially costly errors:

- **Assuming that all homeowners policies are alike.** Actually, policies come in several varieties, and different companies' versions of those varieties differ.

- **Taking it for granted that your insurance company charges about the same premium as others.** Prices, in fact, can differ by astonishingly large margins.

- **Failing to update your coverage periodically.** Even if your policy protects against inflation, the value of your home may outpace it; and as you accumulate more possessions, you may find your personal property dangerously underinsured.

To make sure you have the right protection for your property, review the basic aspects of homeowners policies described in this chapter. They're important to know for another reason, too. Homeowners coverage extends over many areas, some of which seem so unrelated to your house, that you may have overlooked submitting claims for losses you didn't realize were covered.

The basic characteristics of the major types of homeowners policies are summarized on the table on pages 92 and 93. The descriptions are based on standard forms used by insurance companies and the most common amounts of coverage. Each policy type is identified in the table by number (HO-2, and so on) and, in parentheses, by the name often used in the insurance business. One or the other designation should appear somewhere on your policy, although details will differ.

Homeowners policies combine two kinds of insurance.

Coverage for the House and Contents

This part of the policy pays you mainly for losses to the house and related property. And, perhaps much to your surprise, it also entitles you to reimbursement for credit card fraud, forgery and electronic-fund-transfer losses, and for additional living expenses or loss of rental income incurred when you or someone renting part of your house has to move temporarily because of damage to the living quarters.

The coverage on losses other than the house itself are generally figured as a percentage of the coverage on the house. For instance, with HO-2 and HO-3, your personal property is automatically insured for 50% of the house amount. (More coverage is available on many policies—see the discussion of "replacement cost" for household contents later in this chapter.) That 50% is in addition to the insurance on the structure, not part of it. With renters and condominium policies, the coverage depends on how much personal-property insurance you buy.

You can increase some coverages without raising the amount on the structure by paying an additional premium. The special limits of liability that are listed in the table represent the maximum paid for specific items. To get more coverage, you could insure them separately. You can also get additional insurance for a number of items or situations that get limited coverage in a standard policy: off-premises theft; coins, stamps, silverware and guns; business losses; and household help.

Liability Coverage

If your dog bites the mail carrier, or the neighbor's car is crushed by bricks falling from your crumbling chimney, this part of the policy has got you covered—up to a point. Comprehensive personal liability covers damage to property of others and medical payments to others for injuries or damage caused by you or by an accident around your home. Personal-liability coverage kicks in when you are considered legally liable for an injury. It would even pay for legal bills if necessary. To get coverage for medical payments for others, you aren't required to be legally responsible for the injury. You would be covered, for instance, if a visitor tripped over a gap in your front walk and broke an ankle, or if you accidentally beaned someone on the golf course. A typical policy limits personal-liability coverage to $100,000 and medical payments to others to $1,000 per person. You can see that the coverage, though comforting, isn't exactly overwhelming.

Liability coverage typically extends to the policyholder and to family members who live in the house.

How Policies Differ

There are homeowners policies for houses, for condo and co-op apartments, even for renters. The major forms of house policies, called HO-2 and HO-3, offer similar protection on most points. The crucial differences lie in the number of perils your home and property are insured against.

Covered Perils

A homeowners policy will normally compensate you for losses to the building and personal property only if the damage is caused by a peril named in the policy. Other parts of the policy may not apply unless an insured peril produces the loss. For example, all policies pay for emergency repairs to protect the house after an accident, but only on the condition that the damage to the house resulted from an insured peril. This isn't a major worry, because the named perils are pretty comprehensive, but ignorance of your policy can lead to disappointments. No homeowners policy covers damage from floods, for instance. You have to buy that separately.

Not all the policies that insure against a particular peril necessarily provide the same degree of protection, so you have to ask the agent to walk you through the coverage. The HO-3's all-risk coverage on the structure may also include items inside the home; features like wall-to-wall carpet and a built-in dishwasher add value to the house and are often considered part of the structure rather than personal property (as in the HO-2).

If you're considering the HO-3, check whether the risks you are concerned about are covered. The standard HO-3, for instance, won't pay for damage caused by settling, a problem that often concerns homeowners. It also excludes damage from such perils as earthquakes and war (although damage from "civil commotion," such as a riot, is covered). You should buy earthquake insurance if you live in a high-risk area, especially if yours is an older, masonry home or you have much equity invested in it. For this coverage, you have to buy a special add-on, called an endorsement.

When you're looking for a policy to cover items such as pictures, antiques, furs and musical instruments, you might do better by buying additional insurance in the form of riders than by purchasing a homeowners policy with more blanket coverage. The upscale package policies now offered by many companies may provide more coverage than you need, although their prices have gotten increasingly competitive in recent years.

Payback and the 80% Rule

Insurance companies compute payments for homeowners policy losses in two ways. One, called replacement cost, covers what it would cost to rebuild your home if it were totally destroyed or to replace items in it. The other, called actual cash value, takes depreciation into account and pays only the market value of the loss. Thus, your three-year-old television that cost $500 new might be worth only $200 in a cash-value policy. A replacement-cost policy would reimburse you for the cost of a comparable new set.

Because homes are rarely completely destroyed, it's possible to save a little on your premiums by insuring the place for less than it would cost to rebuild the whole thing. As long as the face amount of your policy equals at least 80% of the insurance company's estimated cost to rebuild (excluding the land, which isn't covered), you are fully covered for complete or partial losses—up to the policy's limits. If you have an $80,000 policy on a home the company estimates will cost $100,000 to rebuild and you suffer $10,000 in damage from a kitchen fire, you will be reimbursed for the full $10,000, minus your deductible. If the house burns to the ground and it costs $100,000 to rebuild, your coverage will stop at $80,000.

But insuring for less than full replacement value can be a false economy because of the way insurance companies compensate for partial losses. Say you buy coverage for 80% of the home's value but as prices for labor and building materials rise, that same amount would cover only 70% of the cost of rebuilding. That's seven-eighths of 80%, so for that $10,000 fire, you would get seven-eighths of $10,000 ($8,750) or the actual cash value (replacement cost of appliances and so forth, minus depreciation based on the age of your old appliances).

Even if you insured your home for 100% replacement value a few years ago, you may need to brush the cobwebs off your policy. A policy feature called inflation guard protects you by automatically raising your policy limits in step with rising prices. Insurance agents have access to cost-index figures you can use to help update the replacement value. When you compute the required amount of insurance, remember to eliminate the estimated value of the land, excavations, foundation, underground pipes and similar building components not likely to be damaged.

Replacement-Cost Guarantee

Most major insurers offer a replacement-cost endorsement that will cover all costs of rebuilding or replacing your home in case of a total loss, even if the expense exceeds the amount of coverage you currently carry. This is a feature worth considering if residential construction costs in your area have outpaced inflation in recent years. A typical replacement guarantee comes as part of a 100%-coverage policy and requires you to accept a yearly inflation adjustment and notify the insurer of any additions that might alter the value by more than $5,000.

Replacement-cost coverage for contents

Many companies sell an endorsement that extends replacement-cost coverage to the contents of the place. For an additional premium, some companies will increase the total for personal property from 50% of the insurance on the house to 75%. Endorsements typically exclude fine arts, antiques and other items that are expected to appreciate. They also limit payments for other items to a maximum of four times the cash value.

Insurance for Older Homes

Good as it may be for ordinary homes, the replacement-cost system presents problems for old houses that might cost more to restore to their original condition than to replace using modern materials. Take an old house with a market value of $100,000. It's made with plaster walls and nine-foot ceilings, hand-carved crown molding and so many other nice features that it would cost $160,000 to rebuild. But if you insure this $100,000 home for 80% of its $160,000 replacement cost, or $128,000, the house is overinsured.

That's why insurers have developed special policies for older homes that may be entitled to lower insurance limits based on their market value. Some companies sell them subject to different conditions, and some don't sell them at all. The plans take three forms:

- **A homeowners policy that pays for repairs with less-costly and more-pedestrian modern materials instead of those originally employed** (a parquet floor, for instance, replaced by carpeting over a plywood base). These repair-cost policies generally cost less than other homeowners policies because they cover less.

- **A policy that pays the actual cash value of the loss.** This amount might be interpreted by the company as the current market value of the structure, or its replacement cost minus depreciation.

- **An endorsement—or policy addition—that allows you to insure for less than 80% of the replacement cost of your structure without giving up your right to replacement cost for partial losses.** But for furniture, appliances, awnings, outdoor equipment, clothing and other personal property, the company usually need not pay more than the cash value. If your couch goes up in flames, its value is adjusted for wear and tear.

Finding the Best Deal

Take time to get price quotes from several insurers. You may discover some surprising variations in rates. Differences of 100% for comparable coverage in the same area aren't unheard of. You can't survey all the companies selling insurance in your area, but contacting just a few might produce considerable savings.

There's enough uniformity among the companies' policies that you can use their standard forms to compare premiums. Companies sometimes modify the standard provisions, but it's not always easy to tell whether the changes broaden or narrow your protection, so compare carefully.

You're usually entitled to a lower rate for a brick home than for a frame structure. Also, you might qualify for a discount if your house is new or only a few years old, or if you have installed smoke alarms or antitheft devices.

Be sure to take advantage of differences in deductibles. The base deductible moved up in recent years, from $100 to $250. Consider raising yours further still; many companies will reduce premiums in return for not covering the small losses. However, discount plans are not as common for homeowners insurance as they are for auto policies.

If the insurance agent computes the replacement cost of the house on the basis of its square footage, be sure to check the figures before you agree to the resulting premium.

Take Inventory

It's a good idea to record what you've got in your house so you won't have to rely on memory in case of theft, fire or some other catastrophe. Better yet, walk through the house with a camera or a video camera, carefully scanning each room, plus the garage and outside of the house and yard. Take out the silver and other valuables and photograph them separately. Put the film or videocassette in a safe place—a fireproof safe in the house or a safe-deposit box at the bank.

Making a Claim

Notify your agent or broker of damages as soon as possible. If your losses are covered, he or she will probably arrange to have an adjuster inspect the damages and estimate the repair cost.

If damage from a fire, windstorm or other natural disaster is extensive, you may want to have a public adjuster represent you in filing your claim. Public insurance adjusters are listed in the telephone book.

Don't make any permanent repairs before the insurance adjuster arrives. The company can legally refuse to reimburse you for repairs made prior to inspection.

You don't necessarily have to defer to the insurance company if your claim is refused; policies often allow for varying interpretations. One insurance company adjuster might consider your request for expenses to have someone thaw out frozen pipes an uninsured maintenance cost; another would consider it an insurable peril. Ask for a second opinion, and be persistent.

Don't sign a final settlement agreement if you're dissatisfied with the terms. Accept partial payment to make necessary repairs, as long as the insurer formally acknowledges that it is only a partial

A Guide to Homeowners Policies

These are the principal features of standard homeowners policies.

Policy conditions may vary slightly between companies and according to state requirements.

You can usually increase coverage for some items by paying an additional premium. The special limits of lia-

	HO-2 (Broad Form)	**HO-3 (Special Form)**
Perils (see key below)	1-16	all perils, except those specifically excluded, on buildings
Standard Amount of Insurance on:		
House and attached structures	based on structure's replacement value	based on structure's replacement value
Detached structures	10% of insurance on house	10% of insurance on house
Trees, shrubs, plants	5% of insurance on house; $500 maximum per item	5% of insurance on house $500 maximum per item
Personal property	50% of insurance on house; 10% for property normally kept at another residence, or $1,000, whichever is greater	50% of insurance on house; 10% for property normally kept at another residence or $1,000, whichever is greater
Loss of use, additional living expense; loss of rental unit, uninhabitable	20% of insurance on house	20% of insurance on house
Special limits on liability	money, bank notes, bullion, gold other than goldware, silver other than silverware, platinum, coins and medals—$200; securities, valuable papers, deeds, manuscripts, passports, tickets and stamps, etc.—$1,000; boats including their trailers, furnishings, equipment and outboard motors—$1,000;	
Credit card loss, forgery, counterfeit money, electronic fund transfer	$500	$500
Comprehensive personal liability	$100,000	$100,000
Damage to property of others	$500	$500
Medical payments	$1,000 per person	$1,000 per person

Key to Perils Covered

1. fire, lightning 2. windstorm, hail 3. explosion 4. riots or civil commotion 5. damage by aircraft 6. damage by vehicles not owned or operated by people covered by policy 7. damage from smoke 8. vandalism, malicious mischief 9. theft 10. volcanic eruption 11. falling objects 12. weight of

bility refer to the maximum amounts the policy will pay for the types of property listed. Usually jewelry, furs, boats and other items subject to special limits have to be insured separately if you want greater coverage.

HO-4 (Contents only)	HO-6 (Co-op or Condominium)	HO-8 (Limited Coverage)
1-16	1-16	1-10
no coverage	$1,000 on owner's addtions and alterations to unit	based on struture's market value
no coverage	no coverage	10% of insurance on house
10% of amount of personal property insurance, $500 maximum per item	10% of amount of personal property insurance $500 maximum per item	5% of insurance on house $25 maximum per item
based on value of property; 10% of that amount for property normally kept at another residence or $1,000, whichever is greater	based on value of property; 10% of that amount for property normally kept at another residence or $1,000, whichever is greater	50% of insurance on house; 5% for property normally kept at another residence or $1,000, whichever is greater
20% of personal property insurance	40% of personal property insurance	10% of insurance on house
trailers not used with boats—$1,000; theft of jewelry, watches, furs, precious and semiprecious stones—$1,000; theft of silverware, theft of goldware and pewterware—$2,500; theft of firearms—$2,000		theft on premises limited to 1,000; no coverage for theft of items (named at left) off premises
$500	$500	$500
$100,000	$100,000	$100,000
$500	$500	$500
$1,000 per person	$1,000 per person	$1,000 per person

ice, snow, sleet 13. leakage or overflow of water or steam from a plumbing, heating or air-conditioning system 14. bursting, cracking, burning or bulging of a steam- or hot-water heating system or of appliance for heating water 15. freezing of plumbing, heating and air-conditioning systems and domestic appliances 16. damage to electrical appliances, devices, fixtures and wiring from short circuits or other generated currents payment. If you can't negotiate a settlement, file a written complaint with the company. If that yields no results, you could either enter into arbitration with the company or contact your state's insurance department, which often acts as a referee in such disputes. Only after you've exhausted those avenues should you consider filing a suit against the company.

Other Types of Home-Related Insurance

Title Insurance

Mortgage lenders require you to purchase insurance on the title, which protects the lender's lien on the property against a defect in the title, a lien or some other encumbrance that you didn't know about. To protect yourself, you will have to purchase an owner's title insurance policy.

The difference between the two is that the lender is protected to the extent of the mortgage, which declines as time goes by. You want protection for the price of the house, including your down payment.

Flood Insurance

The federal government is the only underwriter of flood insurance, but most homeowners insurance agents can sell you a federal policy. The average cost is about $350 per year for $100,000 of coverage, with a ceiling of $250,000 on the structure and $100,000 on the contents. You can get details from the Federal Emergency Management Agency (800–427–4661; www.fema.gov).

Umbrella Liability Insurance

Most homeowners or auto policies cover personal liability to just $300,000 or $500,000. Fortunately, you can buy extended personal-liability coverage through what's called an umbrella policy. It picks up where your existing coverage leaves off and protects you to whatever limit you choose. Coverage costs less than you'd think because it pays for claims not completely covered by your other policies and doesn't kick in until that coverage is exhausted. For $1 million worth of coverage you can expect to pay between $125 and $250 per year, but rates and conditions can vary significantly. Make sure you know what's excluded, particularly for business or professional liability.

Chapter 7

Buying a Car

Here's the single most reliable way to save money on cars: Keep your clunker and drive it till it drops. A decently cared-for vehicle should still be running long after the odometer has clocked 100,000 miles. Keep driving it and you save money not only because you don't have to make payments on a new car, but also because insurance premiums are lower, and in some states, so are registration fees. Personal-property taxes are also lower in states that base them on the market value of the vehicle.

Unfortunately, at some point the statute of limitations runs out on this particular money-saving tip. The more the car is in the shop, and the wider the oil slick grows on your usual parking spot, the more you may think seriously about replacing the old chariot with something, well, nicer. Meanwhile, the money you save by not buying a new car tends to be eaten up by the growing cost of keeping the old one on the road.

The question is: Where's the tipping point? When does it become counterproductive to keep laying out cash for old-car repairs instead of new-car payments? To put it another way, how long does it take for the higher cost of *purchasing* a new car to be justified by the growing cost of *maintaining* the old one?

Longer than you think. Runzheimer International, a management consulting firm that specializes in measuring travel and living costs, runs this sort of calculation on a regular basis. Recently it compared ownership costs of a brand-new car against a similar four-year-old car. Both were sensible sedans. The new car was assumed to cost $20,000, financed over four years at 9%. The old car was worth about $4,500 and was assumed to be traded in as the down payment on the new one. The old car has 60,000 miles on it, both cars are driven 15,000 miles per year, and both get 21 miles to the gallon of regular unleaded gas. The box below shows how four years with car payments and low maintenance costs matched up against four years without car payments but higher maintenance costs.

Why Older Is Cheaper

	Old Car	New Car
Mileage at end of four years	120,000	60,000
Total car payments	$0	$18,246
Gas and oil	3,456	3,348
License, registration, taxes	1,347	1,882
Insurance	3,457	3,946
Repairs, maintenance, tires	5,022	2,744
Resale value at end	451	7,408
Total expenses	**$13,282**	**$30,166**
(minus resale value)	–451	–7,408
Total costs	**$12,831**	**$22,758**
Difference		+$9,927

Source: Runzheimer International

The actual numbers are less important than the overriding message: Those loan payments stack the deck against a new car. You could encounter much higher repair costs than assumed and still come out ahead by keeping the old one. If you're confronting this question, you can use the format above to run estimated numbers and see how they come out. Better yet, don't bother. In the absence of a gigantic repair bill—you need a new engine, for example—an old car is almost always cheaper to own than a new one. You can close the gap a bit with a couple of strategies.

Pay cash. This will reduce your total expense by eliminating the interest on the loan, but in order to make a fair comparison you'd also have to take into account what else you might have done with that money and the interest you might have earned if you hadn't spent it on a car. This balancing act is described in the box on page 102.

Pay a lower interest rate. A lower rate helps. But if you eliminated all the interest in the example above, the old car would still be about $6,300 cheaper to own than the new one over the four-year period.

Buy a used car. This is probably your best bet to close the gap completely. The problem is, a used car doesn't come with a new-car warranty, so you take on the same risks of unanticipated high repair bills that you already have with the car you've got.

But let's face it: When all is said and done, most of us don't base decisions on such a detailed accounting of the costs. Comfort, style, image, safety, convenience and reliability—these are the forces motivating the vast majority of Americans who decide to buy a new car. So be it. The important thing is to choose the right car and get to the best possible deal.

Choosing the Right Car

Take some time to consider your choices before you stick a toe in a showroom. Magazine racks are stuffed with new-car guides. Buy more than one to get different perspectives and read about the models that interest you. Use the worksheet on page 99 to sketch out what you want. Show it to the salesperson when you go to the showroom. You might not be able to get every option you want on the car you want, and you may decide that some options aren't worth the added cost. But this list will get you started.

Getting a Good Deal

Once you've decided on a particular make and model, the fun part of buying a new car is over for a while. Now it's time to get down to the business of finding the best possible deal. It will take some work and some hard bargaining. (If you'd like to opt out of the bargaining part, skip right to the section on car-shopping services. If you want to do the haggling yourself, the following are some recommendations for organizing your campaign.)

Set a Target Price
As every car shopper since Fred Flintstone knows, the sticker price on a car is just a suggestion, a place to start. With a few exceptions—the Saturn being the best known—the actual transaction price is set by bargaining, and the better you bargain the better the price you'll get. It helps to have a target price in mind right from the start: a price that gives you a good deal and lets the salesperson make a living.

A number of publications can help you set a target price. Every year the December issue of *Kiplinger's Personal Finance* lists hundreds of new models, with sticker price, dealer cost and target price for each. Other guides are also available. The important thing you're looking for at this point is complete pricing information on all the models you're considering. Your target price will be somewhere between the sticker price and the dealer cost, but keep in mind that you may pay more or less depending on the demand for the car or truck you want. Large dealerships are often in a better position to bargain because they get volume discounts from the manufacturer.

Consider a Clone

You can sometimes find a way to save by comparing similar cars built by different divisions of the same manufacturer. For example, in recent years the Buick Park Avenue, Buick Riviera, Oldsmobile Aurora and Cadillac Seville all shared the same body structure, but their sticker prices ranged from $33,000 to $47,000. Similarly, the Chrysler Concorde and Dodge Intrepid have shared the same underpinnings, but prices have been $1,000 or so apart. The 1998 Toyota Corolla and Chevrolet Prizm were built on the same platform, but the Toyota was priced about $1,000 less.

So-called clone cars aren't easy to spot, and it would be misleading to suggest that the less expensive car has all the goodies of the more expensive one. When you compare clones, ask yourself: Does the extra money buy more performance and durability, or simply a nameplate?

Shop Late in the Month

Many leasing and rebate programs are set on a monthly basis, and are based on dealers making volume sales. Also, dealers must finance the inventory on the lot, and if they can sell cars by the end of the month, they'll save on financing charges. Add to this the fact that most car salespeople have monthly goals or quotas, and you'll find that the last few days of the month can be a good time to buy.

Check Inventories

A rising inventory of cars is worrisome to a dealer, but helpful to a buyer in quest of that particular model. Inventories are measured in terms of "days' supply." When dealers have more cars than they can reasonably expect to sell within 60 days, it's generally considered a buyer's market. You can check inventory in *Automotive News*, a weekly industry publication that is available on some newsstands and in large public libraries.

Look for Incentives

When inventories get high, car manufacturers may begin offering rebates, low-cost financing and subsidized leases. You can find an up-to-date list of incentives in *CarDeals*, a semimonthly publication that typically cites more than 200 deals. Its available from the non-profit Center for the Study of Services, 733 15th Street., N.W., Suite 820, Washington, DC 20005 (800-213-7283); $7.00 per issue). *Automotive News* also publishes the latest rebates each week, and on the Internet rebates and incentives are listed at www.edmunds.com, a Web site sponsored by the company that publishes the Edmund's car-buying guides.

What Do You Want in a Car?

Vehicle type:_____
(sedan, minivan, sport utility, etc.)

Passenger capacity:_____ **Towing capacity:**_____

Check Those Desired

Storage needs:
_____large trunk
_____roof rack

Fuel efficiency:
_____Important
_____Not Important

Drive preference:
_____Rear Wheel
_____Front Wheel
_____Four Wheel
_____All Wheel

Safety features:
_____air bags, front
_____air bags, side
_____anti-lock brakes
_____anti-theft devices
_____extra bumper protection
_____child safety seats

Interior upholstery:
_____cloth
_____leather
_____vinyl

Other options desired:
_____adjustable steering column
_____air conditioning
_____AM/FM radio
_____AM/FM with cassette player
_____AM/FM with compact disc
_____automatic transmission
_____cruise control
_____full-size spare tire
_____power brakes
_____power locks
_____power seats
_____power steering
_____rear-window defogger
_____remote-control mirrors
_____sun/moon roof

Other options desired (list):
_____
_____
_____
_____

Most dealer incentive programs expire around the end of the month, another good reason to shop then. In an incentive program that's based on volume, a dealer can make thousands of extra dollars by selling one more car at the end of the program, even if the sale involves minimal profit.

If you can get a rebate for buying the car you want, it's probably better to use the rebate to cut the price of the car rather than taking the cash. In some states, that will reduce the sales tax on the deal. If you can choose between a rebate and a cut-rate loan, the loan is likely to be the better choice if the car costs more than $20,000. See the table on page 102 for a helpful guide to figuring the angles on such a offer.

Hire Some Help

If you're not confident about your bargaining skills—or if you simply don't like to haggle—you may want to turn to a car-buying service.

Shop Online for a Car

The Internet is a good place to get the latest information on prices, options and other information about both new and used cars. Many sites include a calculator to help you determine loan payments or compare the financing of buying or leasing. Here are a few sites to try:

Microsoft's Carpoint (carpoint.msn.com) has information on options, safety and fuel economy, as well as video tours of car interiors.

Kelley Blue Book (www.kbb.com) provides dealer invoice prices for cars and their options.

Edmund's (www.edmunds.com) provides dealer invoice prices and holdback rates on most cars. (Holdbacks are manufacturers' discounts, which dealers receive after they sell a certain number of cars.)

Intellichoice (www.intellichoice.com) lists the best manufacturers deals available.

AutoSite (www.autosite.com) also has a calculator to work out lease payments.

LeaseSource (www.leasesource.com) contains a wealth of information about leases, including residual values of cars, which are hard to come by. (The residual value of a leased car is the estimated value of the car at the end of the lease.)

In addition, nearly every car and truck manufacturer has a Web site that may offer exact specifications for cars, lists of available options, and financing and leasing information.

CarBargains is an example of this sort of service. For a $190 fee, Car-Bargains (800–475–7283), run by the Center for the Study of Services, in Washington, D.C., will do the legwork for you, getting competitive bids for the car you want from at least five dealers in your area. CarBargains is sometimes able to get lower prices than other car-buying services partly because it receives no money from dealers and thus is working only for you. Dealers pay fees to some other services for the privilege of being the sole dealer the service uses in the area. This really shouldn't matter to you if you get a good deal.

Join a Club

You can join a new-car buying program offered by warehouse clubs such as Costco or Sam's Club and by affinity groups such as credit unions and the American Automobile Association (AAA). If you belong to one of these groups and there's a participating dealer that carries the car you want, you can use the group program to get a discount off the sticker price without haggling. But a shrewd buyer can often beat these prices by a few hundred dollars (or by a lot more if any dealer incentives are in effect).

Club buying programs are typically free to shoppers, but the participating dealers pay the service either a flat advertising fee or a commission on every sale the service steers their way. Because these programs usually work with only one dealer per car line per geographic area, there's no competition. So while the price you get may be a good one, it may not be the best price that's available in your area.

Don't Win the Battle and Lose the War

Be careful not to lose the money you've saved negotiating a good price when you get to the finance and insurance (F&I) office. Here you may confront the offer of a car loan, plus such charges as document preparation, processing, dealer prep and national advertising fees. Dealers see these extras as their chance to win back some of the concessions they made on the price. In addition to those fees, the profits in F&I come from extended warranties, credit life insurance, undercoating, fabric protection, rustproofing and other extras.

Car dealerships put their best salespeople in the F&I departments, so remember the Boy Scout's slogan and *be prepared*. Here's what to know when presented with such extras.

Compare Interest Rates and Rebates

This table lets you compare low-interest financing offered by carmakers with prevailing market rates. The table, which was designed by William Bryan, dean of the School of Business Administration at Loyola University in Chicago, can also help you decide whether low-rate financing is a better value than a manufacturer's rebate.

For example, when prevailing interest rates are 10%, a four-year loan at 6% interest saves you $74.03 for every $1,000 financed. A 4% interest rate saves you $109.75. You save about 23% when you move from a four-year loan to a three-year loan.

What if you're offered a choice: either a 7% interest rate on a four-year loan or a $1,000 rebate? Say you must finance $12,000. Find the 7% dealer's rate under "4-year loan" in the table. If 10% is the market rate, read across the row to 10% and you'll discover that a 7% loan saves $55.84 per $1,000 of the loan, or a total of $670.08 on the $12,000 you want to finance. The $1,000 rebate wins. In fact, you'd have to find a loan at 5% or less to beat the $1,000 rebate. The more money you borrow, the greater the value of the discounted loan. But in this example, you'd have to finance at least $18,000 to beat the savings from a $1,000 rebate.

5-Year Loan (Savings per $1,000 borrowed)

Dealer's Rate	7%	8%	9%	10%	11%	12%	13%	14%	15%
3%	$92.55	$113.81	$134.39	$154.30	$173.57	$192.22	$210.27	$227.76	$244.69
4	69.93	91.73	112.81	133.22	152.97	172.08	190.59	208.51	225.87
5	46.97	69.30	90.91	111.82	132.05	151.64	170.61	188.97	206.75
6	23.65	46.54	68.67	90.09	110.83	130.89	150.32	169.13	187.35
7		23.44	46.11	68.05	89.28	109.84	129.74	149.00	167.66
8			23.22	45.68	67.43	88.47	108.85	128.58	147.69
9				23.00	45.26	66.81	87.67	107.87	127.43

4-Year Loan

Dealer's Rate	7%	8%	9%	10%	11%	12%	13%	14%	15%
3%	$75.67	$93.34	$110.54	$127.28	$143.59	$159.47	$174.94	$190.00	$204.68
4	57.09	75.12	92.67	109.75	126.38	142.58	158.36	173.73	188.70
5	38.29	56.68	74.57	92.00	108.96	125.49	141.58	157.25	172.52
6	19.26	38.01	56.26	74.03	91.33	108.18	124.59	140.57	156.15
7		19.12	37.73	55.84	73.49	90.67	107.40	123.70	139.58
8			18.97	37.44	55.43	72.94	90.00	106.62	122.81
9				18.83	37.16	55.02	72.41	89.34	105.84

3-Year Loan

Dealer's Rate	7%	8%	9%	10%	11%	12%	13%	14%	15%
3%	$58.16	$71.97	$85.49	$98.74	$111.72	$124.44	$136.90	$149.11	$161.09
4	43.82	57.84	71.56	85.01	98.19	111.11	123.76	136.16	148.31
5	29.35	43.57	57.51	71.16	84.54	97.65	110.50	123.08	135.42
6	14.74	29.18	43.33	57.19	70.77	84.07	97.11	109.89	122.41
7		14.66	29.01	43.08	56.86	70.37	83.60	96.57	109.28
8			14.57	28.85	42.83	56.54	69.97	83.13	96.03
9				14.49	28.68	42.59	56.22	69.57	82.66

Financing packages

Often you can find the best loan at the dealership, but in order to evaluate what you're being offered, you'll need to do your homework before heading into the showroom. Call local banks, savings and loans and credit unions for their lowest rates. Be prepared to get your own financing if you don't like the dealer's deal. If you announce your intention to pay cash, don't be dissuaded if an F&I closer presents a computer printout showing that borrowing would be cheaper than paying cash. It would not be cheaper. Customers with marginal credit ratings should be especially wary. You should expect to pay higher rates, but not as high as some dealerships charge. Shop for a loan using the tools described earlier in this chapter.

Document prep and other fees

Dealers are paid by the factory to prepare new vehicles, so if you pay a dealer-prep charge, the dealer gets paid twice. And national advertising is a normal business expense for manufacturers, so it shouldn't be listed on the invoice or added to your final bill by the dealer. (In many states it's illegal for manufacturers to charge dealers for national advertising.)

An invoice charge listed as "local dealer advertising/marketing association" usually represents an actual charge incurred by the dealer to pay for group advertising. The original factory invoice has a box for this item, and the dealer enters the amount, which is typically about 1% to 2% of the invoice price. Dealers consider this to be a legitimate part of their "invoice cost," so if you're being offered a deal that's at or below invoice, you'll probably have to pay it. But if the deal is for a significant amount over invoice, consider this charge to be part of the dealer's gross profit and negotiate accordingly.

Also, beware of last-minute extras such as paint sealant, fabric protection, undercoating, rustproofing and extended warranties.

Extended service warranties

Don't go for these unless you purchase a car with a lot of electronic or computerized gadgets on board. Most extended service warranties never pay out as much as they cost, which gives you some idea of how often they are needed by buyers for serious, expensive repairs. If you do decide on the warranty, review the contract carefully to make sure you aren't paying extra for something already covered by the standard manufacturer's factory warranty.

You don't have to buy an extended warranty the day you buy the car. Most carmakers give you 12 months or 12,000 miles, which should be ample time to see how reliable your car is.

Credit life insurance
This may be the most expensive way in the world to buy life insurance. Unless your health is so bad that you have no other way of protecting your loved ones from debts you leave behind, don't buy credit life.

Rustproofing
Don't buy it, ever. Today's cars are usually warranted by the factory against rust. In fact, the process of rustproofing an already-built car is quite tricky and could be botched, which could lead to more rust and even void the factory warranty.

Fabric protection and paint sealant
These also aren't worth the additional money. Fabric guard can actually stain the fabric and, of course, the factory warranty won't cover any damage that results from this process. You would be better off buying a can of Scotchgard-type spray and applying it yourself. And rather than paying extra for paint sealant, just wax your car from time to time. That should protect it well enough.

The Lure of a Lease

Three things to know about leasing: First, if you like a new car every two or three years and the thought of never-ending car payments doesn't bother you much, then leasing may be a good choice for you. Second, if you plan to purchase your car at the end of the lease, then you'd be better off skipping the lease and buying the car to begin with. Third, to get the best deal on a lease, just as with a purchase, you're going to have to be ready to bargain a bit. And the arcane language of leasing can make the deal harder to judge.

What Goes Into a Lease
The chief lures of a lease are the low or nonexistent down payment, followed by lower monthly payments than you'd have to make if you bought the same car. The reason for this dual blessing is simple: You're paying only for the anticipated depreciation of the car over the

Getting a Fair Deal on a Lease

Monthly payments are less on a lease than if you buy the car but, heck, you're not buying the car. Don't let the allure of lower payments sucker you into paying more than you have to. So what's a fair payment?

This "calculator," prepared with the help of Cedric Rashad, a leasing consultant in Atlanta, will show you. Here's what you need to know to use it:

Capitalized cost. This is the cost of the car written into the lease. Start with your target price or a dealer's quote, and add title and registration fees and other costs, such as taxes or insurance, that will be rolled into the lease.

Capitalized-cost reduction. The total of your down payment, the cash value of your trade-in, and any rebates or discounts.

Residual. The estimated value of the car at the end of the lease. Ask the dealer for this figure or check LeaseSource (see box on page 100). The residual is expressed as a percentage; you can convert it to dollars by multiplying it by the manufacturer's suggested retail price. Manufacturers sometimes subsidize a lease by inflating the residual so you pay for less depreciation.

Money factor. This represents the cost of financing the car. It is the equivalent of an interest rate divided by 24. So if the finance charge is 9%, the money factor would be 0.00375 (0.09/24). Automakers sometimes cut the money factor to subsidize a lease. Ask the dealer for the money factor.

Sales tax. In some states, this tax is charged in full at the beginning of the lease; in others, it's added to each payment. Ask how it works where you live.

Figuring the Lease Payment:
Depreciation

A. Gross capitalized cost (cap cost)	$ _____
B. Cap-cost reduction	$ _____
C. Net cap cost (A − B)	$ _____
D. Residual	$ _____
E. Depreciation (C − D)	$ _____
F. Lease term (in months)	$ _____
1. Monthly Depreciation (E ÷ F)	$ _____

Finance Charge

G. Finance base (C + D)	$ _____
H. Money factor	$ _____
2. Monthly Finance Charge (G x H)	$ _____

Sales Tax

3. Monthly Sales Tax	$ _____
Estimated Lease Payment (1 + 2 + 3)	$ _____

term of the lease—typically two or three years. Thus your payments need to cover only a portion of the car's value.

Take, for example, a nice, new Pontiac Grand Prix, selling for about $20,000. In two years it is expected to depreciate by about 40% of its value, or $8,000. If you lease the car for two years, the dealer will place your payments at a level high enough to cover that $8,000 of depreciation (plus a little profit), plus the cost of the money the dealer borrows to pay for the car in the meantime (plus a little profit), plus charges for this and that, with a little profit tacked on to them, too.

Fortunately, you've got an ally in your effort to sort all this out. The Federal Trade Commission requires that every lease contract disclose the information you need to figure out what you're getting into. It must clearly show:

- **the "capitalized cost"** of the vehicle, (essentially its selling price);
- **any down payment** you'll have to make;
- **registration fees;**
- **trade-in allowances or rebates** built into the deal;
- **interest and other charges;**
- **the exact size of the monthly payment** (including taxes and insurance);
- **the residual value of the car,** meaning its anticipated value at the end of the leasing period;
- **any extra charges or penalties** levied during or at the end of the lease.

The monthly finance charge, which is one important element of the lease subject to negotiation, can sometimes be difficult to interpret. If the dealer uses an *interest factor* or *money factor* instead of the *interest rate*, simply multiply the factor by 24 and you'll have an approximate estimate of the interest rate involved. A factor of .0038, for example, is equivalent to an interest rate of 9.1%.

Finally, the dealer adds sales tax to the depreciation and interest charges to arrive at your lease payment. Make sure when you are comparing leases from one dealer with another that monthly lease payments all include the sales taxes.

How to Negotiate a Lease

The lower the price of the car, the lower your lease payments. That seems obvious, but many people don't realize that they should bargain just as hard on the price as they would if they were buying it. The leasing contract will refer to the "capitalized cost" of the vehicle, meaning price, so set a target price as described in the buying section of this chapter. Some new-car guides, including the annual auto roundup in the December issue of *Kiplinger's Personal Finance,* provide invoice prices and suggest target prices. Some also give expected resale values after two and four years, which can be especially helpful in anticipating the residual value of the vehicle you want to lease. Arm yourself with these figures before you start bargaining and you'll have a better idea whether you have leeway to negotiate a residual value more favorable to you. You want the lowest possible capitalized cost and the highest possible residual value. As a leaser, you're paying the difference.

Other things being equal, the best car to lease is the one that retains more of its value over the term of the lease. If two cars cost the same, you'll pay less to lease the one that depreciates less. This makes luxury cars, which tend to retain more of their value than economy cars, attractive candidates for leasing.

Don't make a down payment if you can avoid it. Though putting more money down lowers your monthly lease payment, why pay the money up front when one of the chief attractions of a lease is that it keeps your up-front outlay to a minimum?

Can you get a better deal if you wait until the end of the model year? This often works for buyers because dealers want to clear off their lots to make room for the new models. But when you're leasing, you're looking for the best relationship between the car's cost and its residual value. (Low cost, high residual, remember?) A car that leaves the lot at the end of the model year is likely to depreciate faster than a car that begins its leased life at the beginning of the year. Once the new cars hit the showroom, you're driving last year's model.

The best leasing deals are usually offered by manufacturers trying to move a particular model. They can lower the cost of the lease by reducing the cost of the car or offering a low financing rate. You'll see lots of great deals advertised, but remember that the terms you see there apply only to that specific model. It pays to shop around.

What You Must Be Told About a Lease

The Federal Reserve Board requires leasing companies to disclose the terms of any consumer car lease in a way that potential customers can understand. Here's an example of what you must be told before you sign. The car in this case has a selling price of $30,000 and the customer is trading in a car worth $4,000.

1. Amount Due at Lease Signing $ 5,799.88
   Itemization of amount due at lease signing
      Capitalized cost reduction $ 5,000.00
      First monthly payment $ 381.44
      Refundable security deposit $ 381.44
      Title fees $ 12.00
      Registration fees $ 25.00
   Total $ 5,799.88
   How the amount due at lease signing will be paid:
      Net trade-in allowance $ 4,000
      Rebates and noncash credits $ 0
      Amount to be paid in cash $ 1,799.88
   Total $ 5,799.88

2. Monthly Payments
   Your first monthly payment of $ 381.44 is due on Jan. 1, followed by payments of $ 381.44 due on the 1st of each month.
   The total of your monthly payments is: $ 13,731.84
   Your Monthly Payment is determined as shown below:
     Gross capitalized cost. The agreed-upon value of the vehicle
       ($ 30,000)
       and any items you pay over the lease term (such as service contracts, insurance) and any outstanding prior loan or lease balance $ 30,000
     Capitalized cost reduction. The amount of any net trade-in allowance, rebate, noncash credit, or cash you pay that reduces the gross capitalized cost
       $ 5,000
     Adjusted capitalized cost. The amount used in calculating your base monthly payment   = $ 25,000

Residual value. The value of the vehicle at the end of the lease
used in calculating your base monthly payment   − $ 13,000

Depreciation and any amortized amounts. The amount charged
for the vehicle's decline in value through normal use and for other items
paid over the lease term   = $ 12,000

Rent charge. The amount charged in addition to the depreciation
and any amortized amounts (also called the "interest.")   + $ 1,300

Total of base monthly payments. The depreciation and
any amortized amounts plus the rent charge   = $ 13,300

Lease term (months)   ÷ 36

Base monthly payment   = $ 369.44

Monthly sales/use tax   + $ 12.00

Total Monthly Payment   = $ 381.44

3. Other Charges (not part of your monthly payment)
    Disposition fee (if you do not purchase the vehicle) $ none
    Annual tax $ 333.00
    Total $ 333.00

4. Total of Payments (the amount you will have paid by the
end of the lease) $ 14,064.84

Early termination. You may have to pay a substantial charge if you end this lease early. The charge may be up to several thousand dollars. The actual charge will depend on when the lease is terminated. The earlier you end the lease, the greater this charge is likely to be.

Excessive wear and use. You may be charged for excessive wear based on our standards for normal use (and for mileage in excess of 12,000 miles per year at the rate of $.025 per mile).

Purchase option at end of lease term. You have an option to purchase the vehicle at the end of the lease term for $ n/a (and a purchase option fee of $_____).

Other important terms. See your lease documents for additional information on early termination, purchase options and maintenance responsibilities, warranties, late and default charges, insurance, and any security interest, if applicable.

Traps to Watch For

Check the lease terms for a "capitalized cost reduction" fee. This is simply another way of asking for a down payment.

Watch out for excess-mileage charges. Dealers want to maximize the resale value of the car when the lease is up, so they limit the number of miles you can drive each year without paying extra. Some leases allow 15,000 miles, but often the allowance is only 10,000 or 12,000 miles per year. If you're likely to exceed the allowance, negotiate for additional miles up front. This can save you a few cents per mile over the end-of-lease mileage charge.

Don't take a longer lease term than you want in a misguided attempt to lower the monthly payments. If you need to get out of the lease before its term is up, you will almost certainly have to pay a steep charge for early termination. Exactly how steep will be spelled out in the contract.

Chapter 8

Insuring Your Car

Accidents happen. In cars, they happen nearly 100,000 times a day, and insurance can be the only thing standing between you and financial catastrophe. The policy describing this protection isn't what you'd call interesting reading. But if you want to know what you are entitled to for your insurance premiums, your policy constitutes the best single source of information.

This chapter opens with explanations of the major parts of a typical policy. The goal is to help you find your way through the thick language still so common there. Later in the chapter, you'll find suggestions for getting the best possible deal on your coverage.

Liability Coverage: In Case You're at Fault

This part of the policy protects you if you (or another person driving your car with your permission) injure or kill someone or damage property.

Assume an accident for which you are clearly responsible: You run a red light, strike another car and injure the driver. Your liability coverage obliges the company to defend you—in court, if necessary—and pay claims to the other driver for vehicle damage and bodily injuries, including medical and hospital costs, rehabilitation, nursing care, and possibly lost income and money for pain and suffering. (The liability section of your policy does not compensate you for damage to your own car or any injuries to you. They are covered by other parts of the policy.)

Now assume that you're involved in a collision at an intersection with no witnesses or evidence to pin the blame on either driver.

Again, under your liability coverage, your insurer agrees to defend you against most proceedings the other driver may take against you.

The company limits its liability payments to the policy limits, or the amount of coverage you select. You can be held personally accountable for any excess.

Liability coverage is mandatory in nearly all states (the others have financial-responsibility laws that can be met by purchasing this coverage). But state requirements are modest—typically $20,000 to $30,000 for bodily injury suffered by one person in an accident, $50,000 for all people hurt in the same accident, and up to $25,000 for property damage resulting from that accident. Alaska, which has the toughest requirements, dictates $50,000 of coverage for one person's injuries, $100,000 for all those hurt in the same accident, and $25,000 for property damage.

How Much Coverage Do You Have?

Insurance companies use a shorthand to describe their liability coverage, and even if you understand the lingo, it might not be immediately apparent how much coverage you carry. The Alaska policy described above, for instance, might be listed as 50/110/25. The first figure refers to the coverage (in thousands of dollars) for injury to one person, the second number is the limit for injuries to all people in the same accident, and the third figure is the coverage for property damage in the same accident. Some companies issue single-limit policies, with one liability limit that applies to total payments arising from the same accident, regardless of the number of people injured or the amount of property damaged.

If the company incurs legal expenses to defend you against a lawsuit, those expenses don't count toward the liability limits. Nor do payments you receive under the policy for bail bonds and earnings lost while attending hearings and trials at the company's request. However, many policies free the company from any obligation to continue your legal defense for sums above the amount it has to pay.

How Much Coverage You Need

You should carry as much liability coverage as you can comfortably afford because damage claims today are sometimes settled for millions. State minimums don't come close to covering the cost of a serious accident. You should carry bodily-injury coverage of at least $100,000 per person, and $300,000 per accident, and property-damage coverage of $50,000, or a minimum of $300,000 on a single-limit policy. Raising your limits isn't expensive: $300,000 in coverage costs 20% more than $100,000, on average. The more coverage you buy, the less you have to pay per $1,000 of coverage. Ask your agent for precise figures. You may even want to investigate raising your liability coverage further through an umbrella policy (see page 94).

Crash Protection

Collision insurance pays for damage to your car, not the other guy's, and it's optional. After all, you can sue someone you think is to blame for damages to your car. So why buy collision insurance, unless you have to (for instance, if you are financing a car)? For a number of reasons:

- **You may be the world's most careful driver**, but it is still possible that you will cause an accident or be held responsible for one. In that case you can't collect for damage to your car from the other driver. Collision coverage will pay for the damage, even if an accident is your fault.

- **You may think an accident is the other driver's fault**, but he may disagree, casting you both into lengthy legal proceedings. With collision coverage, your company can repair the car and take over your claim against the other driver (a procedure known as subrogation). Your company is ethically, but not legally, bound to fight for enough money to pay you back part or all of the deductible.

- **You could get into an accident in which the other driver is clearly at fault** but has no liability insurance. Suing could be pointless. The auto policy's uninsured (or underinsured) motorist coverage does not necessarily pay for damage to your car in this situation. Collision does.

- **Suppose you smash your car into a tree or a telephone pole.** There's no one to sue. Collision will pay for the damage to your car.

The amount of collision coverage your policy provides, and its cost, will depend on your car and its value. Premiums are much higher for vehicles that are expensive, accident-prone, easily damaged, frequently stolen or hard to repair. Those that score well for safety and durability often cost much less to insure. How much you will be paid for an accident depends on the nature and extent of the damage, whether new or refurbished parts are used, and other factors.

However, you should be aware of one special restriction: *The company is obligated to pay only up to the car's cash value.* That means the market value of the car before the accident, minus the salvage value of the damaged vehicle.

For example, say your car was worth $4,000 before the accident and $500 for salvage afterward. The company does not have to pay more than $3,500 in repairs. If the repairs would exceed that amount, the company can take the damaged car and give you the $4,000.

The cutoff for declaring a car to be totaled is usually somewhere around 75% to 80% of the car's retail value, though it may be the cost of repairs plus the car's salvage value. If your car was in the kind of condition that would make it worth more than others of its kind, you'll have a fight on your hands to get what you think it's worth. You don't have to accept the claims adjuster's first settlement offer. Counter with an amount you think is fair. If that fails, take your case to a senior adjuster at the company. Bring your agent in as an ally. Ultimately, you can seek help from your state insurance commissioner, take your case to arbitration, or even file a lawsuit. As your battle gets more and more expensive, you may decide to settle for a somewhat better offer than you got to begin with.

For an extra premium, some insurers will offer replacement-cost coverage for new or recent-vintage cars under the collision (and/or comprehensive) part of a policy. This coverage provides for the full cost of replacing a new or similar car—not just its cash value before the accident—as long as the insurer considers the car not repairable.

Many companies extend their collision coverage to rental cars (provided they are not being used for business). If you are covered, you can turn down the costly collision damage waiver that car-rental agents sell. Check with your insurance agent to find out whether your policy covers rental cars. There are other economical ways to get insurance on rental cars. If you're a member of an auto club, such as AAA, you can get collision protection covering damage to rental cars above a certain amount. Some credit cards provide similar coverage when you charge a rental to them.

Medical Payments: Coverage You May Not Need

If you have coverage for medical payments on your car policy, you and your family members are entitled to reimbursement of medical costs resulting from auto accidents while in your car or someone else's car, or if you're injured by a car while walking or bicycling, regardless of who is at fault. Your guests qualify if they are injured in your car. Medical-payments coverage is typically $1,000 to $10,000 for each person protected by your policy. It would cost you relatively little to raise the coverage to a higher amount.

The company will reimburse a wide range of expenses, from eyeglasses to funeral costs, subject to varying conditions. One policy may pay medical expenses only for the first year after an accident, another for the first three years afterward, and still another up to five years, provided you buy more than a stipulated amount of protection. Payments may be reduced by any amount that you receive or are entitled to receive from other parts of the policy or from other sources. In certain situations the company may pay only expenses that exceed the compensation obtainable from other insurance.

Before you consider additional medical coverage, check to see if it would duplicate coverage you already have under other medical policies, especially comprehensive, high-limit health insurance.

Protection Against Uninsured and Underinsured Drivers

Despite laws requiring auto insurance in practically every state, a lot of people are driving without any—or without enough—liability insurance. The uninsured/underinsured motorist section of your policy protects you if you or family members who live with you are hurt by one of those drivers while you're in your car, walking or, in some policies, bicycling. Your guests also qualify if they are hurt while in your car. This coverage also applies when you are struck and injured by a hit-and-run driver and, in some cases, by a driver insured by a company that becomes insolvent.

In order for this coverage to kick in, the other driver has to be declared at fault. In most states, when blame is in doubt or the amount payable is contested, you and your insurer have to submit your differences to arbitration. This kind of insurance usually covers only costs arising from bodily injuries. In states in which property damages are included, claims may be reduced by a deductible.

Generally, companies are obligated to pay claims up to the minimum amount fixed by your state for liability insurance. But often you can purchase higher limits for an additional premium.

Most states require insurance companies to offer uninsured or underinsured coverage; some companies combine them. If your company offers them separately, buy both.

Comprehensive Coverage

A combination of liability, collision, medical payments and uninsured/underinsured motorist insurance would seem to take care of all conceivable risks. Yet none of that insurance would necessarily cover losses to your vehicle from these hazards: theft of the car or some of its contents, collision with an animal, glass breakage, falling objects, fire, explosion, earthquake, windstorm, hail, water, flood, malicious mischief, vandalism or riots. Comprehensive insurance, which is optional, will cover those losses, usually up to the car's cash value and sometimes subject to a deductible.

In some areas, if you keep your car in a garage or off-street parking area or if the car has a good antitheft device—for instance, one that prevents the car from being started—you can get a reduction in your comprehensive-coverage premium.

Comprehensive coverage also entitles you to some compensation for renting a car if yours is stolen. Check your policy to see how much the policy would pay per day and for how long; different companies pay different amounts, subject to state requirements.

No-Fault Insurance

Liability insurance is your main financial defense against catastrophic damage you might cause to others or their property. But it's not always clear who's to blame for an accident, and proving fault, when it is possible, can entail delays and expensive legal action. Meanwhile, the victims may not get paid.

Enter no-fault insurance, an attempt to take the fault out of liability. The idea is to have accident victims' medical expenses paid by their own insurance companies, regardless of who is to blame for the accident, thereby eliminating the costs and delays of legal actions.

Plans that reduce the fault element in some way have been enacted in about half the states and the District of Columbia. Some of those states have adopted "add-on" plans that increase the benefits you can obtain from your own insurance company but do not restrict your right to pursue a liability claim. No-fault laws vary greatly, but

Insurance Shopping Guides

If you live in one of the following states, call for a free copy of its latest premium survey. Most states include quotes for several hypothetical drivers in different areas of the state. While you might not exactly fit the profile of the hypothetical drivers, you can see which insurance companies offer the lowest premiums in your area.

Alaska	800–467–8725	Michigan	877-999-6442
Arizona	800–325–2548	Minnesota	800-657-3602
Arkansas	800–852–5494	Missouri	800–726–7390
California	800–927–4357	Nevada	775–687–4270
Connecticut	800-203-3447	New Jersey	800–446–7467
Delaware	800–282-8611	New York	800–342–3736
District of Columbia	202–442-7770	North Dakota	800–247–0560
		Oregon	503-947-7980
Florida	800-342-2762	Pennsylvania	877-881-6388
Hawaii	808–586–2790	South Carolina	803-737-6180
Illinois	217–782–4515	Texas	800–252–3439
Kansas	800-432-2484	Utah	800–439–3805
Kentucky	800–595–6053	Vermont	802-828-3301
Louisiana	800–259–5300	Virginia	800–552–7945
Maine	800–300–5000	Washington	800–562–6900
Maryland	800–492–6116	Wisconsin	800–236–8517

they do tend to have some elements in common.

- **Your insurance company pays you and others covered by your policy** for medical bills, lost wages, the cost of hiring people to do household tasks you are unable to perform as a result of injuries, and funeral expenses up to specified limits.

- **No-fault plans don't pay for property damage.** This is covered by other parts of the policy.

- **No-fault plans don't pay for pain and suffering.** For that you have to be able to sue someone.

- **You usually can't sue others until expenses of the type covered by the no-fault insurance exceed a certain level.** By the same token, you are immune to suits by others until their costs exceed that limit.

To protect themselves against fault-based suits permitted under no-fault regulations, drivers in some states must also buy traditional liability insurance. But liability payments may be reduced by compensation received under the no-fault provisions. Add-on no-fault plans generally provide benefits similar to, but less generous than, the pure no-fault programs, and the injured person has the right to sue for pain and suffering.

How Your Rate Is Set

If you have lots of accidents or tickets for moving violations, you're going to pay more for auto insurance. Everyone knows that. But the way companies sort out the good risks from the bad aren't so obvious. When you apply, you're screened by a company underwriter who decides whether the company wants to insure you and, if so, in what general category to place you.

Who Are You?

The insurance company starts with a set of base premiums for each of the coverages that make up its standard policy. Those base rates are set to cover a particular customer: an adult male with a standard car used only for pleasure. Everyone else pays more or less, depending on the company's evaluation of his or her relative risk potential.

In effect, you're assigned to a group defined by characteristics believed to predict the group's chances of creating insurance losses. Although classification plans differ, the companies employ for the most part these basic criteria: age, sex, marital status, accidents and traffic violations, the number of cars being insured, the models, use of the cars (pleasure, commuting, business, farm), mileage expected, whether a young driver has taken a driver-education course, and whether he or she is entitled to a good-student discount. Some even take your credit record into account.

Each characteristic is assigned a numerical weight based on its tendency to increase or reduce the probability of loss. All the factors that apply to you are combined to fix your position on the company's premium scale. A ranking of 100 indicates that you pay 100% of the base premium. With a 90 ranking you pay 90% of the base, which means you are getting a 10% discount. If you're pegged at 225, you are charged 225% of the base.

Where Do You Live?

Each company periodically computes the premium income it needs in each state in which it operates. It wants enough money to pay for claims and expenses, and a margin for profits and contingencies. The total state premium is then allocated among the various territories into which the state is divided for rating purposes. The boundaries are supposed to demarcate areas with significantly different loss records.

The exact relationships vary from one state to another, but according to one study, people in central neighborhoods of small metropolitan areas (100,000 to 400,000 population) generally pay less than the state average; their counterparts in big cities (over one million) pay substantially more. Small-city suburbanites are charged less than the state average; big-city suburbanites are charged somewhat more.

Are You a Good Driver?

A company may separate drivers into three underwriting categories: preferred, standard and nonstandard. Its rates for preferred applicants generally run 15% lower than standard rates. Nonstandard policyholders are charged anywhere from 35% to 75% more than standard rates, depending on the number of accidents they've been involved in and, in many cases, the number of traffic violations.

If you're considered a high-risk driver, you might be rejected and eventually forced into a state-assigned risk plan that requires a regular insurance company to give you protection—at a price that may be at least 50% more than other drivers are charged. Alternatively, one of the regular companies might shunt you into a subsidiary company that specializes in high-risk drivers. Those "substandard" insurers, as they are known in the business, also charge higher premiums.

Getting a Good Deal

Auto-insurance premiums have long since reached big-ticket status, so it pays to look for opportunities to keep your costs down and still have enough protection.

Do Some Homework

Arm yourself with as much information as you can before you call companies. It's fairly easy to get cost, coverage and deductible information from auto insurers; it's much more difficult to find out their financial stability and service record—things you'd be interested in knowing if you get a good cost quote from a company you're not familiar with. You can check out stability in *Best's Insurance Reports:*

Discounts to Ask For

1. Multi-car and multi-policy. It often pays to insure your home and all of your family's vehicles with the same company. Families with teenagers at home who drive their own cars can usually save 15% to 20% by insuring all the vehicles and drivers on one policy. (New drivers seeking individual policies, on the other hand, are frequently referred to state-run "assigned-risk plans," which have high premiums.)

You can have the company assign drivers to particular cars your family owns. The rate will go down if your insurer assigns your highest-risk family member (the youngest, newest or most accident-prone driver) to the family's oldest, least valuable car.

2. Anti-theft devices. This discount applies to comprehensive coverage only. Not all car alarms and security devices are equal in the eyes of insurance companies, so check with your insurer before you have an anti-theft system installed.

3. Safety features. Some insurance companies give discounts for safety features, such as air bags. Don't expect a windfall, however. Discounts will take only a few dollars off—maybe $8 to $10. A few states require insurers to offer discounts for anti-lock brakes. But in other states some companies have stopped giving these discounts because they say anti-lock brakes have not reduced claims.

4. Carpooling. Commuting mileage drives up your insurance premium more than non-commuting mileage. All ten of the leading insurers polled by the Insurance Information Institute offered a 15% to 20% discount to commuters sharing driving responsibilities in car pools so they don't drive their cars to work every day. You can also save by using public transportation.

5. Good driver. If you avoid accidents and traffic violations through safe, sensible driving, you'll be rewarded handsomely with lower rates. Good-driver discounts range from 10% to 20% of the total premium. You may also get a discount if you or another family member complete a defensive driving course, or if your teenage son or daughter completes high-school driver's education.

6. Nonsmoker. If you or a family member quit smoking, it could lower your car insurance premium as well as your homeowners and life insurance premiums.

7. Good student. If you have a teenage driver, you may be eligible for a discount of 5% to 25% if he or she gets good grades at school.

8. College student. Alert your insurance company when a son or daughter goes away to college, whether he or she takes along a car or not.

Property-Casualty at your local library; insurers with the top two ratings can be considered solid. (You can also ask an agent how A.M Best, the rating service that publishes the guide, rates his or her company.)

Many state insurance offices keep track of consumer complaints and will share the results if they're asked. (See the box on page 117.) Finally, read your policy carefully so that you're sure of the kind and amount of protection you have.

Compare the Premiums

Survey after survey confirms that auto-insurance companies often charge greatly different premiums for the same coverage. In New York, Pennsylvania and elsewhere, premiums have been shown to vary sometimes by more than 100%.

Rates may not vary as wildly in your area, but the odds are you will find substantial differences if you get premium quotes from several companies. Begin with a market leader, such as State Farm or Allstate, and use that quote as a measure against which to judge identical coverage at other companies. Many state insurance offices distribute auto-insurance pricing guides, but the categories they use may not match yours. Use such a guide to identify your state's most cost-effective insurers. Then get price quotes from a handful and you'll have a truly comparative guide.

Manage Your Teenagers' Driving

Young drivers pay much more than most others because, as a group, they have more accidents. Rates will drop several notches when they reach age 25 or marry. But meanwhile, avoid letting them be the principal driver of a car, which pushes up the premium even more. Most companies give good-student discounts to young drivers—commonly 5% to 25% off for a consistent B average—because statistically, good students are superior drivers. Young drivers can also get discounts for completing an approved driver-training course. Parents of students who attend school more than 100 or 150 miles away from home (and away from the family car) may also get a break.

Drive Carefully Yourself

Discounts are common for safe-driving records: Some companies give 5% off for drivers with three years of a clear record, raising the discount to 10% for drivers with six or more accident- and violation-free years. Depending on which company insures you and where you live, you may even get a discount if you're a nonsmoker, a woman who is a household's only driver, a senior citizen, or a member of a certain profession (such as law or medicine) that is statistically less accident-prone. All ten of the leading insurers polled by the Insurance Information Institute offered a 15% to 20% discount to commuters sharing driving responsibilities in car pools, meaning they don't drive their cars to work every day. When comparing policies, consider discounts but don't fixate on them. A discount may very well be offset by a higher premium to begin with.

Check Your Car's Rating

Insurers charge more for cars with high claims rates, no matter how good the driving record of the owner. Some charge less for collision and comprehensive coverage on models that score well for safety and durability, but add surcharges for others. A surcharge or a discount isn't a judgment of a car's quality. The rate variations reflect repair costs, accident frequency, theft losses and other factors.

Before you buy your next car, it might pay to check on such differentials. The Insurance Services Office provides a rating service used by hundreds of insurance companies, and your agent should be able to tell you the new car's rating. Or, get free loss data on nearly 200 makes and models by requesting the Highway Loss Data Institute Composite chart from the Insurance Institute for Highway Safety, Publications Dept., 1005 N. Glebe Road, Arlington, VA 22201; www.hwysafety.org or 703–247–1500. Loss data do not necessarily translate into discounts, but they do show which vehicles are most likely to qualify.

Consider Raising Your Deductibles

It might make sense to choose the highest deductible you can afford to pay without seriously disrupting your finances. The idea is to pay for affordable damage yourself and let insurance kick in for bigger losses. Whatever your situation, you can save something by accepting a larger deductible and thus transferring part of the risk from the company to yourself. It's not an ideal solution, but it's one of the few cost-cutting opportunities that are readily available. By raising your collision deductible from $100 to $500, for instance, you might be able to cut your collision premium almost in half.

Reduce the Coverage on an Old Car
You could consider dropping comprehensive and collision coverage on an old car to reduce your insurance costs fast. That would expose you to additional risk, but remember that the insurance company won't pay more to fix a car than it's worth. Each year's depreciation therefore diminishes the maximum claim you can make against your collision coverage. If your car is five or more years old, depending on its value, you may be better off dropping both collision and comprehensive coverage and banking the savings. Estimate your car's value by studying the classified ads or by consulting used-car price guides, and consider how much protection you're really buying for your collision and comprehensive premium.

Insure All Cars With the Same Company
You get a break for the second and successive cars covered by the same policy, so it's usually more economical to put all your cars on one policy. Similarly, consider using the same company for other policies. Some insurers offer discounts of up to 10% if you cover both your car and your home with them.

Don't Pay by Installments
The company tacks an extra amount on to your premium when you pay in monthly or quarterly installments. If you can afford it, pay your premium in a lump sum.

Chapter 9

Paying for College

Colleges and universities occupy a favored place in the American economy. Normally a steadily rising price for a product or service attracts a fresh supply of it to the marketplace, and the competition serves to discourage the price increases. But in the marketplace of higher education, the supply stays about the same. Result: Prices rise higher and higher and there's nothing anybody can do about it.

Perhaps that's oversimplified. Perhaps one day one of your children will write a doctoral thesis that does a better job of explaining this phenomenon. First, though, you've got to get them through school, and that's going to take money—lots of money.

Take heart: millions of parents pay only part of their kids' college costs. The rest is covered by money that students save or earn, and by scholarships, grants and loans, many of them subsidized by the government. But most government aid programs are based on financial need, and the money to fund them runs out long before everyone's needs are met. If college is just around the corner, jump to the sections later in this chapter that describe ways to improve your chances of getting some of that aid.

If college is still some years away, your best strategy is to assume you'll qualify for no aid and start salting away the dollars you'll need. How many dollars is that? Well, colleges, like cars, clothes, and other modern necessities, don't all cost the same. Community colleges and many state colleges and university systems might even be described as bargains. A very useful guide to financial aid, *Don't Miss Out*, by Anna and Robert Leider (Octameron Associates), reports that average annual tuition at community colleges runs about $1,500. At state universities, the average is $3,000. Most

What College Will Cost in the Future

This table will help you figure out how much total annual college costs are likely to rise, taking into account increases during the college years. If your child begins school in two years, for instance, add the annual cost of years two through five to get an estimate of the four-year cost. If she is an infant, add years 18 through 21. Use the $36,000 starting point if you have your eye on an elite private institution, the $11,000 starting point for in-state costs at public schools, and the $25,000 starting point if you're not sure. If you're starting early, bear in mind that the further out you go, the tougher it is to predict how quickly college costs will rise. As the years pass, you'll want to look into how much college costs are really rising and adjust your planning accordingly.

Today	1 Year	2 Years	3 Years	4 Years	5 Years	6 Years	7 Years
$36,000	$37,800	$39,690	$41,675	$43,759	$45,947	$48,244	$50,656
25,000	26,250	27,563	28,941	30,388	31,907	33,502	35,177
11,000	11,500	12,128	12,734	13,371	14,040	14,742	15,479

Today	8 Years	9 Years	10 Years	11 Years	12 Years	13 Years	14 Years
$36,000	$53,189	$55,848	$58,640	$61,572	$64,651	$67,884	$71,278
25,000	36,936	38,783	40,722	42,758	44,896	47,141	49,498
11,000	16,253	17,066	17,919	18,815	19,756	20,744	21,781

Today	15 Years	16 Years	17 Years	18 Years	19 Years	20 Years	21 Years
$36,000	$74,841	$78,583	$82,512	$86,638	$90,970	$95,518	$100,294
25,000	51,973	54,572	57,301	60,166	63,174	66,333	69,650
11,000	22,870	24,014	25,215	26,476	27,800	29,190	30,650

private schools charge around $13,000 on average. Room, board, books, travel and so forth can add several thousand dollars.

Those are today's costs, of course. They'll be higher in the years ahead. The table above shows what increases of 5% per year will do to the cost of four years of college with current *annual* costs of $36,000 (high), $25,000 (medium) and $11,000 (low) over the next 18 years.

How can you possibly pay bills like that? Well, maybe you can't, but before you give up, consider how much of the cost you may be able to accumulate in the time you have available to do it.

The table on page 126 shows how much you'd have to set aside each month in order to accumulate $10,000 over various periods of time assuming various rates of return. (These are after-tax rates, but the effect of taxes may be negligible if you use one or more of the tax-favored investment vehicles described later.)

Chapter Nine • **125**

Read down the left-hand column until you come to the number of years you have left before college starts. Then read across to the number that lines up under the percentage figure that you think represents a reasonable rate of return. If you're going to accumulate the money in your checking account (not the recommended way to save) choose 3% as your rate. If you're wedded to bank CDs and U.S. savings bonds, choose 5%. If you don't know what rate to assume but are willing to follow conservative suggestions, choose 10%.

Let's say you've got ten years to go and hope to earn 10%. Those

How Much Do You Need to Save?

Use this table to determine how much you need to save per month for each $10,000 of college expenses.

Years	3%	4%	5%	6%	7%	8%	9%	10%	11%	12%
1	$820	$815	$811	$807	$802	$798	$794	$789	$785	$781
2	404	400	395	391	387	383	379	375	371	367
3	265	261	257	253	249	245	241	237	234	230
4	196	192	188	184	180	176	173	169	165	162
5	154	150	146	143	139	135	132	128	125	121
6	127	123	119	115	112	108	104	101	98	95
7	107	103	99	96	92	89	85	82	79	76
8	92	88	85	81	78	74	71	68	65	62
9	81	77	73	70	66	63	60	57	54	51
10	71	68	64	61	57	54	51	48	46	43
11	64	60	57	53	50	47	44	42	39	36
12	58	54	51	47	44	41	39	36	33	31
13	52	49	45	42	39	36	34	31	29	27
14	48	44	41	38	35	32	30	27	25	23
15	44	41	37	34	31	29	26	24	22	20
16	41	37	34	31	28	26	23	21	19	17
17	38	34	31	28	25	23	21	19	17	15
18	35	32	29	26	23	21	19	17	15	13
19	33	29	26	24	21	19	17	15	13	11
20	30	27	24	22	19	17	15	13	12	10
21	29	25	22	20	17	15	13	12	10	8

columns intersect at $48, meaning you'll have to devote $48 a month to your college investment plan in order to come up with $10,000 in 10 years. If $50,000 is your goal, you'll have to set aside five times as much, or $240 a month. If that's more than you can afford, then adjust your goals. If you can afford more, go for it.

Where to Stash Your College Cash

The kinds of investments that can help you accumulate a college nest egg are the same that can help with other investment goals. But because you need a plan designed specifically to pay for college education, there are a few twists and turns to take into account.

To begin with, any plan you set up should be easy and economical to fund on a regular basis. Stocks with dividend reinvestment plans, for example, are ideal if they also permit you to make additional purchases on a regular basis for a small fee or no fee. Mutual funds with high front-end loads would be unsuitable if you have to pay the load each time you add to your holdings. By the same token, no-load funds are ideally suited for a college investment plan.

Your college portfolio should contain a diversified mix of investments. If you have at least eight to ten years to go, stocks or stock-oriented mutual funds should form the core because stocks historically have paid the highest returns over long periods. As you get within four years of the student's first year at college, sell enough of the stocks or stock funds to pay for freshman year. Put the proceeds where you may earn less but can be certain that the money will be there when you need it—a money-market fund, for instance. Leave the rest of the investment fund in stocks and repeat the exercise as you draw within four years of the sophomore year of college, and so forth. Following are some instruments especially suited for college savings plans.

Zero-Coupon Bonds

Zeros get their name from the fact that they pay no interest at all until maturity. This lack of income along the way means that zeros must sell at a huge discount from face value in order to attract any investors, and the further away the maturity date, the bigger the discount must be. A $1,000 zero-coupon bond yielding 7% and maturing in five years would sell for $705. A 7% zero maturing in ten years would go for a bit under $500. The same bond maturing in 15 years would sell for about $350.

This sort of predictable payout makes zeros ideal for a conservative college-savings plan because the maturities can be timed to coincide with the year college bills come due. On top of that, zero-coupon Treasury bonds come with no risk of default.

There is a catch, however. Even though zeros pay no interest each year, at tax time you have to act as if they do. As the "phantom" interest accrues year by year, you must pay income tax on it. This heads off a big tax bill at maturity, but it's a pain in the neck to pay tax today on income you won't see for years. Zero-coupon municipal bonds, which pay tax-free interest, are the surest way around this annoyance. In addition, there may be a way to take advantage of the so-called kiddie tax to minimize the damage from a taxable zero.

The kiddie tax is a provision of the law that says children under the age of 14 must pay tax at their parent's rate on any "unearned" income—such as interest, dividends or capital gains—to the extent that it exceeds a certain level, $1,400 for year 2000. A child's first $700 of income is tax-free. The next $700 is taxed at the child's rate. Any investment income above $1,400 is taxed at the parent's rate. (These thresholds may change with inflation.)

Assume that the child's rate is 15%, which is the lowest tax bracket, and the parent's rate is 28%. Clearly you have much to gain by shoveling the maximum amount of interest into the child's bracket. And, in fact, the way the IRS says zero-coupon bond interest must be reported works to your advantage.

Say that you, the child's grandparents, or all of you together buy your newborn a $10,000 zero paying 9% and maturing in 18 years. You pay $2,050 for it. The interest the bond earns each year isn't one-eighteenth of the $7,950 difference between the purchase price and the maturity price. Because of compounding, the interest is lower in the early years than it is in the later years. In the first year, $2,050 earning 9% compounded semiannually earns about $190. That gets added to your principal, so that in the second year the bond pays 9% of $2,240, or $200. The third year you'd earn $230, and so forth.

As you can see, your child can earn a lot of interest before incurring any tax at all. Because of the accelerating nature of the interest payments, a large part of the taxable buildup will occur after the child turns 14 and is taxed on all income at his or her own rate, probably 15%.

U.S. Savings Bonds

Savings bonds that you use to pay college bills for your kids offer some tax advantages that help to compensate for the rather puny interest they pay. The interest can be entirely tax free under certain circumstances. First, the bonds must be purchased in the parents' names. Bonds purchased in your child's name don't qualify for the tax-free feature. Second, you must be at least 24 years old at the time of purchase. Third, you must use the bond interest to pay tuition or fees. You can't use the money for room and board, books, transportation, or other personal expenses.

There's a catch that prevents some parents from benefiting from Uncle Sam's limited largess. At the time you redeem the bonds, what's called your "modified adjusted gross income" can't exceed $81,100 if you're married, or $54,100 if you're single when you redeem the bonds. (Modified adjusted gross income includes the interest on the bonds.) Above those levels, the allowance is phased out gradually until it disappears completely at incomes exceeding $111,100 for married couples and $69,100 for single parents. (These figures were for 2000, and will be adjusted to keep pace with inflation.)

Tuition Savings Plans

State-sponsored tuition savings plans come in two varieties, and the differences are important. *Prepaid-tuition plans* guarantee participants that if they pay the price of tuition today—in a lump sum or in monthly installments—the state will cover the cost of tuition at state colleges and universities when their child is ready to attend years from now. At recent count, most states offered such a plan or were planning to launch plans with D.C., Georgia and South Dakota the only holdouts. (Their residents can use plans in other states.) *College savings plans* are, in effect, state-sponsored investment accounts. Money is invested by the state, and participants share in the earnings of the account.

Both kinds of plans offer significant tax advantages. Earnings aren't taxed at all by the state, and federal tax isn't due until the money is withdrawn, and then it's taxed at the student's rate. (In Mississippi and New York, participants can deduct their contributions to the plan from their taxable state income.)

Beyond that, the plans are quite different. As a practical matter, prepaid-tuition plans pay a rate of return equal to the inflation rate at public colleges and universities in your state. That can be attractive when tuition inflation is running at 10% or so. It's a lot less appealing when the rate is 5%, which is what it has been in recent years. The main attraction here is the guarantee that college bills will be covered.

The rate of return on college savings plans depends on how good a job the state's money managers do with the funds they invest. There's usually no guarantee, meaning you could actually lose money.

You can't really shop around for the best plan, since you're pretty much stuck with what your state offers. (Exceptions: Any U.S. resident can participate in the plans sponsored by Colorado, Massachusetts, New Hampshire, New York and Utah, although only state residents get the state-tax advantage.) Before deciding whether to commit your child's college fund to such a plan, examine the prospectus with the following questions in mind.

What if your child decides to attend a private college or an out-of-state college?

Money in a college savings plan can be used at any accredited college in the country. Prepaid-tuition plans are sometimes less flexible. You may pay a penalty for using the money at a school not covered by the plan.

What if your child decides not to go to college?

Both kinds of plans will generally transfer the account to a sister or a brother with no penalty, but if the money is not used to pay for college at all, you'll pay a heavy price. Some plans simply refund your principal without crediting the earnings, and may even charge a fee.

What is the effect of the account on eligibility for financial aid?

The money in a prepaid-tuition plan reduces your calculated need dollar for dollar. College savings plans, on the other hand, are counted just like any other investment, meaning that your need will be reduced by 5.6% of the balance if included in your assets, or 35% of the balance if included in the student's assets.

Education IRAs

If you meet the income tests, you can put up to $500 (increasing to $2,000 after December 31, 2001) a year into an Education IRA for any child under age 18. You can't deduct the contribution, but your account grows tax-deferred, and if you use withdrawals to pay college expenses, they are completely tax-free.

You're eligible to make the full $500 contribution if your adjusted gross income is less than $150,000 on a joint return ($95,000 on a single return). You can make partial contributions with AGI up to $160,000 and $110,000, respectively. The income limits apply to whoever funds the account, which doesn't have to be the student's parent.

That's the good news. That bad news is that there are some traps lurking in education IRAs that can make them less valuable than they seem. In any year that you tap an education IRA for college costs, you forfeit your right to a Hope Scholarship tax credit or a Lifetime Learning credit (see below and page 132). What's more, the education IRA account could be considered the child's asset under financial-aid formulas, which would reduce the amount of financial aid you might receive. The law also prohibits funding an education IRA in the same year that you contribute to a state-sponsored prepaid tuition program.

The Roth Alternative

If you know you'll have a child in college when you reach age 59½, then forget the education IRA and put your college savings in a Roth IRA instead. You can contribute up to $2,000 a year to a Roth IRA—four times as much as permitted by the education IRA. (Contribution limits will increase to $3,000 from 2002-2004; $4,000 from 2005-2007; and $5,000 in 2008. They will be indexed for inflation after that.) Once the account has been open for at least four calendar years after the year it was begun and you are 59½ or older, you can withdraw as much as you want, tax- and penalty-free. Younger parents can withdraw the money they've contributed to a Roth without paying tax or the 10% early-withdrawal penalty. If you dip into earnings, that amount will be taxed. But as long as the money is used for college bills, there's no early-withdrawal penalty.

When College Bills Are Due

Most people need some help with college bills, and Congress devised a couple of new programs of college credits to provide that help.

Hope Scholarship Credit

This is the more valuable of the two. It permits you to subtract from your tax bill 100% of the first $1,000 you pay for tuition and fees (but not room and board) and 50% of the next $1,000. The Hope credit applies only to the first and second year of college, but you can claim it for as many of your children as qualify.

Lifetime Learning Credit

This takes up where the Hope credits leave off. The Lifetime Learning credit is 20% of the first $5,000 of higher-education costs, for a maximum credit of $1,000 per year. You just lop the qualifying amount off your tax bill. It can be used after the freshman and sophomore years and you can even use it for yourself if you return to school. But you may claim only one Lifetime Learning credit per year, regardless of how many students in your household qualify for it.

If your adjusted gross income exceeds $40,000 on an individual return or $80,000 on a joint return, you begin to lose your eligibility for the Hope and Lifetime Learning credits. Eligibility disappears completely at $50,000 and $100,000 respectively, where the phase-out zones end. Within the zones, you qualify for a partial credit.

Careful timing of your tuition payments can maximize the benefit. Say, for instance, that your child's final college semester begins in January. If you pay the bill in late December, you'd have no qualifying payments in the following year. Postponing the payments until January buys you an extra Lifetime Learning credit worth as much as $1,000.

Getting Financial Aid

The quest for financial aid begins with a form: The FAFSA (Free Application for Federal Student Aid) will determine your fate at most public schools and even some private colleges. Colleges that offer their own sources of aid may also require a Profile form, which asks for additional data. Both forms are available from your child's high school guidance office or the college's financial-aid office. You can also get them online, at www.fafsa.com.

The FAFSA demands detailed information on your income and assets as well as your child's. Forms must be filed in January or February of your child's senior year in high school. The government processes your data and generates your "expected family contribution" to college costs. In other words, based on what you put on the form (plus some corroborating paperwork), the government decides what you can afford to pay. It's probably more than you think it should be.

Armed with this official assessment, the college will assemble your financial-aid package. But you're not finished yet. Although the feds don't count home equity and money in retirement accounts when calculating your estimated family contribution, many private colleges do, and they'll adjust your contribution accordingly. A financial-aid officer may also make adjustments for private-school tuition for younger siblings, unusually high medical expenses or a recent job loss.

You can expect your notification of financial aid in the spring—usually following on the heels of college acceptance letters. Most aid packages are a combination of grants, scholarships and loans, with a growing emphasis on loans in recent years.

Protecting Your Assets

The process seems cut-and-dried, but there are a few perfectly legal moves you can make to minimize your income and assets, and thus maximize your chances for aid. FAFSA measures your income and assets beginning in January of your child's junior year in high school, and ending in the fall of her junior year in college. Therein lies the key to your campaign. Before January of your child's junior year in high school:

- **Try to get bonuses paid early**—perhaps your employer will issue you a check on December 31 of your child's junior year in high school instead of January 1.

- **If you're going to sell stocks, mutual funds or any other appreciated property** to pay for college, complete the sale before the magic date so that the profits won't boost your income during the crucial years.

More income- and asset-reducing ideas:

- **Postpone IRA distributions until after the financial-aid years.** IRAs don't count as an asset, but the withdrawals will count as income.

- **If you own your business, consider purchasing business equipment during the financial-aid years.** You can deduct up to $20,000 in the year you purchase the equipment, which will serve to lower your business income.

- **Don't overwithhold from your paycheck for state and local taxes.** Any refund will have to be reported on your federal income-tax return and will boost your income the following year.

- **If you were planning to purchase a computer or new car, do it before sending in your FAFSA form.** You might also consider spending money in a custodial account for your child's college computer or a car for the college years if these are expenses you would have incurred anyway.

- **If grandparents (or other relatives) are going to contribute to the college bills, ask them to pay the college directly,** rather than giving you the money. FAFSA doesn't request information about contributions from family members. (However, the Profile aid form does ask for that information and will factor it into your expected family contribution.)

Sources of Aid

Financial-aid packages are typically made up of grants, loans and perhaps a job for the student. Most of this money comes from the

---

Student Loans at a Glance

Loan rates (in parentheses) are as 2001-2001. They are effective on loans disbursed after July 1, 1998.

Federal loans	Borrower	Interest rate	Fees	Term
Stafford	student	91-day T-bill + 2.3 points (6%)	4%	10–30 years*
Perkins Loan	student	5%	none	10 years
PLUS Loan	parent	52-week T-bill + 3.1 points (6.8%)	4%	10–30 years*

Private loans Type	Borrower	Interest rate	Fees	Term
Nellie Mae EXCEL	parent	prime + 0.75 to 2 points (7.5% to 8.75%)	2% to 6%	4–20 years
Sallie Mae Signature Loan	student	prime + 0 to 2 points (6.75% to 8.75%)	0% to 6%	up to 20 years
TERI Alternative Loan	parent or student	prime rate minus 0.5 points (6.25%)	5% to 6.25%	up to 25 years

*The ten-to-30-year repayment term reflects special extended payment options, but ten years is the standard term.

federal government, and from the school's own resources. The only way to discover what's available is to apply for it. You can get information about school-based programs from the schools you're interested in. You can get information about federal programs from high school guidance counselors, college financial aid officers or from the Federal Student Aid Information Center (800–433–3243). Here's a run-down of major sources of federal assistance.

Pell Grants

These go to the neediest students, ranging up to about $3,300 for 2001-2002 but often a lot less. To qualify your child for a Pell grant, your FAFSA must show a big shortfall between the cost of college and the amount your family can afford to pay.

Federal Loans

Stafford loans

These low-interest loans go to students, not parents, and are subsidized or unsubsidized, based on need. With a subsidized Stafford, the federal government pays the interest until six months after the student leaves college. With an unsubsidized Stafford, the borrower can defer payments on principal and interest until after graduation, but the government won't pick up the tab.

Stafford loans are guaranteed by the federal government and usually made by banks, although some come directly from the government itself, through the school. They can be as much as $2,625 for freshmen, $3,500 for sophomores, and $5,500 per year for juniors and seniors. Independent students and graduate students can borrow more. Interest rates are adjusted annually to equal the rate on a 91-day Treasury bill plus 2.3 percentage points, capped at 8.25%. Borrowers pay a 4% loan fee up front, which is deducted from the loan amount. Ten years is the usual payback period.

Perkins loans

Perkins loans come through the financial-aid offices and are limited to students with significant financial needs. They carry a super-low interest rate of only 5%, and payments are deferred until nine months after graduation. Certain jobs after graduation could also result in the cancellation of some or all of the debt. For example, if your child becomes a teacher in a low-income area, a law enforcement officer or a Peace Corps volunteer, the government might repay the loans for him. The borrowing limit is usually about $4,000 per year, although the school has the option of setting a higher limit.

PLUS loans (for Mom and Dad)

These loans are made directly to parents. Though you must have a good credit history to qualify, you can borrow just about whatever you need to meet college expenses. The interest rate is the 52-week Treasury-bill rate plus 3.1 percentage points, but it can't go any higher than 9%. Repayment begins 60 days after the lender pays the school, but you can opt to pay only interest while your child attends college. Lenders include banks, credit unions and other financial institutions, as well as some colleges.

Private Loan Sources

You could borrow money for college from non-college-related sources, of course. Following are some nongovernment sources of loans designed especially for the parents facing college bills.

Nellie Mae's Excel loans

Through Excel, you can borrow the money you need to cover the cost of college less any financial aid you've been awarded. The interest rate is the prime rate plus 0.75 percentage point in the first year and prime plus 2 points in the remaining years. To qualify, you need a clean credit report for the past two years, and your debt payments (including your mortgage and the Excel loan) can't exceed 40% of your gross monthly income. There's an up-front fee of 7%, which goes into an insurance fund to cover defaults. (Contact Nellie Mae at 800–367-8848, or at www.nelliemae.com.) Nellie Mae also makes Stafford and PLUS loans.

PLATO

If you're creditworthy, you can borrow between $1,500 and $25,000 a year and take up to 15 years to repay a PLATO loan. The interest rate is 7.9% in the first year, and prime plus 3.5 points thereafter. The up-front fee is 8% of the loan amount. (Contact University Support Service at 800–467-5286 or at www.plato.org.)

Sallie Mae
Sallie Mae, the Student Loan Marketing Association, offers what it calls Signature Loans for up to the full cost of college, minus any financial aid you have received. The interest rate is variable, based on the 91-day Treasury bill rate plus 3.1 percentage points or 3.5 points (depending on whether a parent co-signs the loan). A 6% up-front fee is subtracted from the proceeds you receive. If your child has a Stafford loan with a lender participating in the Signature Loan program, then all your loans can be consolidated into one account, and you may qualify for discounts if you make your payments on time. (Call Sallie Mae at 800–891–4595 or visit its Web site at www.salliemae.com.)

The Education Resources Institute (TERI)
TERI offers loans through banks for the full cost of college less any amount you're awarded for financial aid. You must qualify for the loan and meet the same qualifications as for a Nellie Mae loan. Rates are between prime and prime plus 2 percentage points. You'll be charged a 5% origination fee, which can be added to your loan balance. For information call 800–255–8374 or visit its Web site at www.teri.org.

In Quest of the Elusive Scholarship
For help in finding a privately sponsored scholarship, talk with your high school guidance officer and college financial-aid officers to get ideas and applications. You should also spend an afternoon at the library looking through the scholarship guides. Information is, of course, also available on the Internet. Try the College Board's at www.collegeboard.com or fastWeb at www.studentservices.com/fastweb. Other good sources of scholarship information include your employer, professional associations, unions, local civic groups, state agencies, unions, religious groups, and advocacy organizations for ethnic groups or people with disabilities.

Chapter 10

A Comfortable Retirement

Let's call it the Great American Retirement Income Challenge and divide it into two parts: 1) How much money will you need to live financially worry-free when you retire? 2) Where will you get it?

How Much Will You Need?

When you retire, you'll tend to spend less on clothing, commuting, Starbucking and other daily expenses associated with earning a living. If you have kids, they'll probably be on their own, freeing up a big chunk of your income.

Unfortunately, other expenses have a way of taking up the slack. For instance, studies show that retirees spend significantly more on health care—no surprise there. They also spend more on gifts, household maintenance and other things. All this makes the Great Retirement Income Challenge especially—well, challenging.

Some estimates hold that you can keep your standard of living with as little as 40% to 60% of your preretirement income. Yeah, right. Maybe Michael Jordan could get by on that, but chances are your income is a little less than his, so you'd better plan on replacing a higher proportion of it. In fact, 75% or 80% might be a more realistic neighborhood. On top of that, even though inflation has been tame for several years now, it's still true that a dollar of income tomorrow won't be worth as much as a dollar of income today. The bottom table on page 145 lets you estimate inflation's impact on your future income.

Where Will You Get It?

So where will you get that kind of money? It will probably come from a combination of places: social security, a pension plan perhaps, and your own saving and investing. Before you try to devise a way to generate the do-it-yourself portion of the nest egg, you need to estimate how much retirement income you can reasonably expect from pensions and social security. The worksheet on page 141 will help you do just that.

Your company's human resources or benefits office can give you the information you need about future pension payments, and a call to the Social Security Administration (800–772–1213) will get you a form called "Request for Earnings and Benefits Estimate Statement." About a month after you return the completed form, you'll get an estimate of your future benefits, which you can use in the worksheet. The Social Security Administration offers benefits estimates online. You can check your estimated benefits—as well as get a wealth of information on social security—at www.ssa.gov.

What Your Money Will Be Worth in the Future

This table shows how much your current savings and investments will be worth in the future, assuming various annual rates of return. It also can be used to calculate how inflation will affect your living expenses. Say you plan to retire in 20 years and expect your investments to grow 10% a year between now and then. Find 20 years in the left-hand column and 10% on the horizontal scale across the top. The place where the two columns intersect shows a multiplier of 6.73. That tells you that $1,000 in your retirement account today will grow to $6,730 in 20 years, assuming a 10% annual return (6.73 X $1,000 = $6,730).

But in 20 years, you'll need more than $1,000 to have the purchasing power of $1,000 today. How much more? First make an assumption about inflation—4% a year is a reasonable estimate for the next 20 years. Where the 4% column intersects with 20 years, the multiplier is 2.19. That means that you'll need $2,190 in 20 years to match the purchasing power of $1,000 today.

Years	Rate of return								
	4%	5%	6%	7%	8%	9%	10%	11%	12%
10	1.48	1.63	1.79	1.97	2.16	2.37	2.59	2.84	3.11
15	1.80	2.08	2.40	2.76	3.17	3.64	4.18	4.78	5.47
20	2.19	2.65	3.21	3.87	4.66	5.60	6.73	8.06	9.65
25	2.67	3.39	4.29	5.43	6.85	8.62	10.82	13.59	17.00

If you plan to retire before age 62, you can't count on all your long-term savings and investments to contribute income right from the start. The worksheet reflects the fact that employer pension benefits are rarely available before age 55, that social security benefits can't start before age 62 and that IRA funds are generally tied up until age 59½.

How to Use the Worksheet

The worksheet assumes that you want to live on 80% of your preretirement income and that you'll be able to earn 8% per year on the investment assets you build between now and then without depleting your capital. (The 8% assumption about earnings is lower than the assumption you should make while building capital, because it reflects the fact that once you are retired, you'll want to keep your money in lower-risk investments that produce a high level of income.) Odds are that you'll have to dip into capital on some sort of regular basis.

Now begin to plug in your numbers.

Savings and investments

Begin with what you have in your retirement fund today and use a future-value multiplier from the table on the previous page to see what it will be worth in the future. If you have $50,000 now, you plan to retire in 15 years, and you expect your savings and investments to yield 6% a year after taxes, multiply $50,000 by 2.4—the figure where the 15-year row and 6% column intersect. That's $120,000. If the nest egg generates 8% a year, you can count on it for $9,600 toward your retirement needs.

Equity in your home

This line assumes that you will use your home equity as a source of income—either by selling your home and renting or by "buying down" to a smaller place and investing the freed-up equity to generate income. Begin with the current value of your house and apply a future-value multiplier from the table on page 139 to estimate its value when you'll sell it. If you don't have a feel for where values are headed where you live, use 4%. Subtract any mortgage you'll still have outstanding at that time and enter the result on line 2. Since Congress has declared that the first $250,000 of profit from the sale

> # Where Will the Money Come From?
> **A: Your Goal:** Current income x multiplier from table on page 139
> x 0.80 = $_____
> **B: Anticipated resources at crucial ages:**
>
> | | Current value x Multiplier from table, Page 139 | 50-54 | Age 55-59 | 60-62 | 62+ |
> |---|---|---|---|---|---|
> | Resource | | | | | |
> | 1. Investments | $_____ x 0.08 =$____ | $____ | $____ | $____ | |
> | 2. Equity in home | _____ x 0.08 = ____ | ____ | ____ | ____ | |
> | 3. IRAs* | _____ x 0.08 =XXXX | XXXX | ____ | ____ | |
> | 4. Keoghs | _____ x 0.08 =XXXX | ____ | ____ | ____ | |
> | 5. 401(k)s | _____ x 0.08 =XXXX | ____ | ____ | ____ | |
> | 6. Pensions** | _____ | XXXX | ____ | ____ | ____ |
> | 7. Social security** | _____ | XXXX | XXXX | XXXX | ____ |
> | Totals | _____ | ____ | ____ | ____ | |
> | Shortfall (A minus B) | $_____ | $____ | $____ | $____ | |
>
> *You can withdraw your own contributions to a Roth IRA penalty-free before age 59½
> ** When they become available, your pension and social security benefits form the cornerstone of your retirement income. It's assumed you will not be investing them.

of a home is tax-free—$500,000 if you file a joint return—it's highly unlikely that taxes will cut into your profit.

Individual retirement accounts
Consider this money tied up until you reach 59½, although there are exceptions. Apply a future-value multiplier from the table to the current value of your IRAs (and other resources, too).

Keogh accounts
You can tap a Keogh without penalty starting at age 59½ (age 55 if you close the business funding the plan), with the same exceptions as you get in an IRA. Complete this line the same as you did line 3.

401(k) and profit-sharing plans
Money in employer-sponsored 401(k) and profit-sharing plans can be withdrawn without penalty as early as age 55 if you leave the job. If you roll over a distribution into an IRA—to avoid paying all the tax at once—the money will be controlled by the IRA rules.

Employer-paid pension benefits

Outside of the government and military service, defined-benefit plans rarely pay anything before age 55. Your personnel office should be able to estimate what you can expect and when you can start collecting it. You can probably count on your benefits increasing for each year past age 55 that you delay retirement, provided you stay with the same employer. If you leave that company, your pension will almost certainly be frozen at the level you had earned before leaving. If you have a defined-contribution pension plan, the value of your account would probably keep growing after you left because you would keep it invested.

Social security benefits

You can't collect social security retirement benefits before age 62, and if you choose to begin at that age checks will be reduced to 80% of what you'd get if you waited until 65 to start collecting. The age for receiving full benefits and the reduction for early retirement will increase gradually beginning in the year 2000. Use the estimate you requested from the Social Security Administration to complete this line.

What If You Come up Short?

Completing the worksheet almost certainly generates bad news: a substantial shortfall that makes retirement look like a swan dive into poverty. In a sense, the worksheet is stacked against you because it is based only on the growth of what you've accumulated so far and does not take into account any future savings.

Say you're hoping to retire in 20 years, and you face an annual shortfall of $24,000, or $2,000 a month. Use the first table on page 145 to calculate the size of the nest egg it will take to generate that much income for a given length of time. If you'll need the extra $2,000 a month for 30 years, for example, your additional nest egg must total $272,560, if you assume it will earn 8% a year after you retire. That means you'll have to invest enough over the next 20 years to total $272,560 when you retire.

(A mathematical footnote: A nest egg of $272,560 may not seem to be enough to generate an income of $2,000 a month if it earns 8%, because 8% of $272,560 is only $21,804, which amounts to $1,817 per month. The apparent discrepancy is explained by two factors: First, the unexpended portion of the nest egg continues to earn interest, so drawing out $2,000 per month depletes the fund by something less than $2,000. Second, the schedule assumes that you will exhaust the fund in 30 years, so it's okay to nick the principal a little each month.)

How Much Time Do You Have?

You can use the table below to figure out how much extra you need to start saving each month to accumulate your retirement fund. Assuming a 10% annual yield, you can see that $100 a month invested over 20 years will build a nest egg of $76,570 ($10 a month invested for 20 years at 10% = $7,657 x 10 = $76,570). Dividing the amount you need—$272,560—by that figure gives you 3.6. Multiply that by 100 and you can see that you need to sock away $360 a month over the next 20 years to meet your goal.

Fortunately, that's not necessarily an *extra* $360 a month. Part of it may be covered by money you are already putting away in IRAs and other plans, plus future contributions by your employer to a job-related account. Also, the amount you need to come up with yourself probably drops as the years go by and other retirement income kicks in. If you needed the extra $2,000 a month for five years instead of 30—to tide you over for the years between an early retirement at age 50 and age 55, perhaps—the monthly savings required over 20 years would drop from $360 to $129.

What kinds of investments offer the best hope of achieving your retirement goals? A core portfolio of individual stocks (or stock-oriented mutual funds) is ideal for a long-term goal such as retirement. Other chapters in this book describe how to go about selecting them. In general, the more time you have, the more risk you can afford to take.

How $10 a month will grow

Years	8%	9%	10%	11%	12%
10	$1,842	$1,950	$2,066	$2,190	$2,323
15	3,483	3,812	4,179	4,589	5,046
20	5,929	6,729	7,657	8,736	9,991
25	9,574	11,295	13,379	15,906	18,976

If Retirement Is 20 or More Years Away
With 20 years or so to go, an aggressive-growth mutual fund would be appropriate for a portion of a portfolio dominated by growth stocks (or funds that specialize in them); zero-coupon bonds (especially zeros sheltered in IRAs and other retirement plans; well-selected real estate; and other long-term investments.

If Retirement Is Ten Years Away
There's still plenty of time to recover from market reversals, but it's also time to think a little more conservatively. Market peaks present opportunities to move money out of risky aggressive stocks and into dividend-paying growth stocks with reinvestment plans. You can give your mutual fund portfolio a less risky profile by moving into growth-and-income, equity-income and balanced funds. At this point in your life, consider moving about 20% of your portfolio into cash, meaning money-market funds, certificates of deposit with various maturities, and Treasury bills. You give up the chance that a soaring market will reward you, but you also give up the risk that a plunging market will punish you.

If Retirement Is Only Five Years Away
When you get to within five years of retirement, it's important to be conservative, but it's also important to remain diversified. Hang on to some growth stocks or growth-stock funds, especially those that pay good dividends. If interest rates look high, buy bonds; if rates decline, you'll have the choice of selling them at a profit or keeping them for the high income they provide. If you own rental real estate that has appreciated in value, look for opportunities to take the gain so you can move the money into a more liquid investment that will produce more income in retirement.

Numbers You'll Need to Plan Your Retirement

The first table shows how large a fund you'd need to yield $100 a month over a number of years when invested at various rates. Let's say you needed the money over 20 years during which you can earn 9%, you'd start with $11,114 (where the 20-year and 9% columns meet). To generate $500 a month, you'd need five times that amount, or $55,570.

You can also use this table to find out what you'd get monthly from a hunk of cash you'll draw down over your retirement. Say you have $250,000, on which you figured you could earn 9% over 20 years. Tracing the 20-year and 9% columns gives you $11,114—the amount that will yield $100 per month. Your fund is 22.5 times greater, so your payout would be 22.5 times greater than $100, or $2,250 monthly.

The second table shows how much you'd have to save monthly at various interest rates over a number of years to accumulate $1,000. For example, to build your kitty over 20 years by investing in a 9% account, you'd need to save $1.49 a month. To accumulate $55,000, you'd need to save 55 times $1.49, or $81.95.

The last table shows what inflation can do to your retirement expenses. Start with your estimated expenses for your first year of retirement. To see how they'd grow after five years of 5% inflation, find where those columns intersect and multiply your original expense figure by the number shown there.

How Much Capital You'll Need to Yield $100 a Month for the Period Indicated at Interest Rate Indicated

Years	5½%	7%	8%	9%	10%	11%	12%
5	$ 5,235	$ 5,050	$ 4,932	$ 4,817	$ 4,706	$ 4,599	$4,496
10	9,214	8,613	8,242	7,894	7,567	7,260	6,970
15	12,238	11,125	10,464	9,860	9,306	8,798	8,332
20	14,537	12,898	11,955	11,114	10,362	9,688	9,082
25	16,284	14,149	12,956	11,916	11,005	10,203	9,495
30	17,612	15,030	13,628	12,428	11,395	10,501	9,722

Monthly Investment Needed to Accumulate $1,000 over the Period Indicated at Interest Rate Indicated

Years	5½%	7%	8%	9%	10%	11%	12%
5	$14.45	$13.89	$13.52	$13.16	$12.81	$12.46	$12.12
10	6.24	5.76	5.43	5.13	4.84	4.57	4.30
15	3.57	3.14	2.87	2.62	2.40	2.18	1.98
20	2.29	1.91	1.69	1.49	1.31	1.14	1.00
25	1.55	1.23	1.04	0.89	0.75	0.63	0.53
30	1.09	0.81	0.67	0.54	0.44	0.35	0.28

Inflation's Effect on Your Figures

Years	3%	4%	5%	6%	7%	8%	9%	10%
5	1.16	1.22	1.28	1.34	1.40	1.47	1.54	1.61
10	1.34	1.48	1.63	1.79	1.97	2.16	2.37	2.59
15	1.56	1.80	2.08	2.40	2.76	3.17	3.64	4.18
20	1.81	2.19	2.65	3.21	3.87	4.66	5.60	6.73
25	2.09	2.67	3.39	4.29	5.43	6.85	8.62	10.82
30	2.43	3.24	4.32	5.74	7.61	10.06	13.27	17.45

Chapter 11

Passing It On

Writing a will is a sobering act that's easy to put off, which is probably why so many of us never get around to it. But consider for a moment what might happen if you don't leave clear instructions for the distribution of your property after you're gone.

If you die without a valid will, the state will supply a ready-made one devised by its legislature. Like a ready-made suit, it may fit—and it may not. Abraham Lincoln died without a will, and his estate was divided (as an estate still would be in some states) into a third for his widow and a third for each of their sons. One son was grown and the other was 12 years old, so the arrangement may not have been considered ideal by Abe's widow, Mary.

The possibilities for trouble when you leave no will are nearly endless. A hostile relative might be able to acquire a share of your estate, for example, or a relative who is already well-fixed might take legal precedence over needier kin.

So you should have a will, a carefully written one. Oral wills, the procrastinator's deathbed solution, aren't legal in a number of states and are valid only in narrow circumstances in states where they are legal. Handwritten, or holographic, wills are legal in some states but can create complicated and expensive problems for the people you leave behind. Videotaped wills may make good drama on television, but they have no legal standing in the real world.

Six Steps to a Good Will

This is not a time to take shortcuts in the hope of saving a few bucks. It makes sense to pay a competent lawyer a reasonable fee to write a document that will lay out your wishes and stand up later to scrutiny by the probate court, your beneficiaries and anyone you choose not to make a beneficiary. Will-writing kits, on paper or computers, can help you focus your thinking and get ready to meet with the lawyer.

(Our personal favorite is the kit you'll find in *Kiplinger's Home Legal Advisor*, helpful software published by Block Financial Corp.) Getting a good will also takes some thinking on your part.

1. Size Up Your Estate
Start by drawing up a list of your assets—real estate, bank accounts, stocks, bonds, cars, boats, life insurance, profit-sharing and pension funds, business holdings, money owed to you, and the like.

2. Protect the Children
If you have minor children, you'll have to decide who you want to take care of them if you and your spouse both die. This involves setting up a guardianship, a task that has two principal functions. The first is to provide for the proper care of the children until they reach the age of majority. The second is to manage the money and property you leave to the children and distribute it to them as you would wish.

The same person could fill both roles, but the "guardian of the person" can be different from the "guardian of the property." Pick the former for his or her nurturing abilities, the latter for financial knowledge and money-management skills. If you're divorced, you might be inclined to choose a separate property guardian because the surviving parent typically gets custody of the children. Name backup guardians in case your first choice dies, is incapacitated or perhaps wants to relinquish the job after a few years.

In addition to your will, it helps to leave detailed instructions on how you want your children raised. In a letter, or even on videotape, you can spell out anything from your views on cars and part-time jobs for teenagers to your priorities on education and religion. These instructions can provide important guidance, but they aren't binding.

3. Distribute Your Property
Next you'll have to decide how you want your estate distributed. This is obvious and straightforward in many instances, such as leaving everything to your spouse, or to your children if both of you die. You needn't account for every piece of jewelry or every stick of furniture (but do account for pets). Making specific bequests of long lists of items like that in a will can needlessly complicate matters and lead to extra costs and delays. Write these up separately and let your executor carry out your instructions.

4. Choose an Executor

You'll have to be prepared to name an executor (sometimes called an administrator), whose job it will be to see to the distribution of your estate and make sure any taxes, debts and other obligations are paid.

Choose your executor carefully. Naturally, he or she should be someone you trust—a relative, a friend, your lawyer, anyone you feel is able to take on the responsible task of disposing of your estate. The person should be willing to do the job, so check before you name someone who might later refuse, thus forcing the court to appoint someone you might not have chosen.

A husband and wife can name each other or a mutually agreed-on person as executor for their wills. You'll also have to choose someone who will step in as executor if for some reason your first choice can't do it.

5. See the Lawyer

For simple wills a generalist should be able to do the job at a reasonable price. If your estate is substantial, consult a lawyer who specializes in estate planning. Don't conclude hastily that your estate is too small for you to worry about taxes. Insurance policies, company benefits, investments and home equity could make your estate larger than you think it is.

Depending on where you live, the complexities of the document you need and the time you've spent sorting things out already, the lawyer's fee can range from as little as $300 or so for a simple will to $200 an hour for the time involved in planning a complex estate. There is no such thing as an average price.

6. Change It If You Want

If your situation changes in the future, you can always amend the will. Under some circumstances, you *should* change it, as described in the box on page 152. But don't do it yourself. You could invalidate the entire document in the eyes of the court, thus undoing the good you've done so far. Go to the expense of having the lawyer make the changes.

(It is possible to change your will *too* much, however. Jack Kent Cooke, the late owner of the Washington Redskins, revised his will frequently, writing people in, then writing them out again. All these changes, plus a complex personal life, seemed likely to tie up his will in legal battles for years to come.)

How Large Is Your Estate?

Although you don't have to pay any federal estate taxes until your taxable estate exceeds $675,000, you might be surprised by all the things the government counts in getting there. ($675,000 is the threshold for 2000 and 2001. It will increase to $1 million in 2002, and ultimately to $3.5 million in 2009.)

In the worksheet below, the ownership column is included because how you own property is pivotal to how much of its value will be included in your estate when you die. In the "value" column, include the following:

- the full value of property of which you are the sole owner;
- half the value of property you own jointly with your spouse with right of survivorship;
- your share of property owned with others;
- half the value of community property if you live in a community property state.

Also include the value of the proceeds of an insurance policy on your life if you own the policy, your vested interest in pension and profit-sharing plans, and the value of property in revocable trusts.

Assets	Value	Who Owns It
Cash in checking, savings, money-market accounts		
Stocks		
Bonds		
Mutual funds		
Other investments		
Real estate		
Personal property, including furniture, cars, clothing, etc.		
Art, antiques, collectibles		
Proceeds of life insurance policies you own on your life		
Pension and profit-sharing benefits, IRAs, etc.		
Business interests: sole proprietorship, partnerships, closely held corporations		
Money owed to you, such as mortgages, rents, professional fees due		
Other		
Total Assets		

Liabilities		
Mortgages		
Loans and notes		
Taxes		
Consumer debt		
Other		
Total Liabilities		

Net Estate (total assets minus total liabilities) **Net Estate** _____

Once your will is written, don't just stuff it in a safe-deposit box. The box may be sealed after your death, making the document unavailable for a time. Perhaps you can keep it in the lawyer's vault or safe at home with your other important papers. You may also want to give a copy to the executor or the principal beneficiary. Subject to your lawyer's advice, consider including a letter of last instructions that will help your executor gather your affairs together and carry out your wishes.

Estate-Planning Basics

Everything you own is considered part of your estate when you die. To grasp the importance of planning for the distribution of your worldly goods, consider all the things that influence what happens to them.

The Role of Probate
This is the procedure by which state courts validate a will's authenticity, thereby clearing the way for the executor to collect and pay debts, pay taxes, sell property, distribute funds and carry out other necessary tasks involved with settling an estate. The process can be slow and expensive, and probate fees can absorb as much as 10% of the estate's assets.

Mindful of criticism and the spread of devices designed expressly to keep assets out of the grip of probate courts, most states have adopted a streamlined procedure for small estates. About half the states have informal procedures requiring little court supervision. Sometimes all that's necessary is for the appropriate person to file an affidavit with the court and have relevant records, such as title to property, changed. Formal probate, in which major steps along the way are supervised by the court, is commonly reserved for large estates.

Not all of your estate has to go through probate. Among the items exempted from probate—but not necessarily from taxes—are life insurance payable to a named beneficiary, property left in certain kinds of trusts, and assets such as homes and bank accounts held in joint tenancy with right of survivorship.

Joint Ownership

Property that is jointly owned with a right of survivorship—the form that is commonly used by married couples but can be employed by any two people—automatically passes to the other owner when one owner dies. Tenancy by the entirety, another form of joint ownership, can apply only to married couples and isn't recognized in all states.

Federal Estate and Gift Taxes

In 2000, an estate had to amount to more than $675,000 before it incurred any federal tax at all. This threshold is scheduled to rise on an intermittent schedule until 2009, when it will reach $3.5 million. Under certain circumstances, owners of family farms and small businesses (defined as those whose business accounts for at least half of their estates) get a $1.3-million exemption, but this will become unnecessary when the basic individual tax exemption rises to $1.5 million in 2004. And married couples who leave personal property to their spouses can avoid tax on the entire estate of the first spouse to die, no matter how much it's worth. This is called the "marital deduction."

If your estate crosses the threshold, the pain is intense for your heirs. Federal estate-tax brackets *start* at 37% and climb in fairly rapid order to 55%, which applies to estates over $3 million, although here, too, there will be some relief—the top tax bracket will drop to 45% by 2007. Americans who have accumulated substantial assets during their lifetimes need to be careful that they don't hand most of it over to Uncle Sam when they die.

Before you die, you can give away up to $10,000 a year to as many recipients as you want without incurring what's called a gift tax. For married couples the limit is $20,000. The gift tax is designed to prevent people from giving away much of their wealth to prospective heirs, thus escaping the estate tax entirely. The gift- and estate-tax schedules are the same and range from 18% to 60% of the taxable amount, reaching the top bracket for taxable gifts or estates over $10 million. These schedules will remain the same until 2004 when the estate tax exemption will continue to rise and the gift tax exemption will remain at $1 million. (In truth, few people, even big gift givers, ever pay any gift tax. Instead, a gift large enough to trigger it takes a nick out of the estate-tax credit, thus boosting the tax after the death of the gift giver.)

There is no limit on gifts between spouses and no limit on the marital deduction described above. This means that, with proper estate planning, the marital deduction and the estate-tax exclusion can be used to pass estates of any size from one spouse to the other without incurring any federal estate tax. To make sure that you take full advantage of this opportunity and to minimize estate taxes upon the death of the second spouse, consult with an experienced estate attorney familiar with the laws of your state.

Your State Wants a Share, Too

The federal government is not the only authority wanting a piece of your estate when you die. Most state governments levy some form of death taxes that cut into much smaller estates than the federal tax does. The most commonly imposed state levy is an inheritance tax. An inheritance tax is paid by each heir out of his or her inheritance unless the will directs that the estate cover it. (This makes an inheritance tax different from an estate tax, which must be paid by the estate before its proceeds can be divided up among the heirs.) Most states also have a so-called pickup tax, which applies only to estates owing a federal tax. While the pickup tax doesn't actually increase your tax, it claims for the state an amount that would otherwise be claimed by the feds.

Seven Reasons to Change Your Estate Plan

After you've created your will and an estate plan, you'll most likely need to revisit them at key points in your life as your circumstances change.

- You Get Married
- You Become a Parent
- You Approach Middle Age
- You Get Divorced
- You Remarry
- You Retire or Move to Another State
- Your Spouse Dies
